THE
CHALLENGE
OF
JESUS

THE
CHALLENGE
OF
JESUS

by John Shea

The Thomas More Press

Copyright © 1975 by the Thomas More Association.
ISBN: 0-88347-053-5

TO MY FAMILY
AND FRIENDS

TABLE OF CONTENTS

Preface

The only excuse (a lame one at that) for another book on Jesus is that we are never quite through with him. When the last syllable of the last word about Jesus the Christ has been spoken, a small, balding man who until now has been silent will say, "Just a moment I. . . ." After two thousand years people still journey to Jesus. They bring a vaunting ego and last year's scar, one unruly hope and several debilitating fears, an unwarranted joy and a hesitant heart—and ask Jesus what to make of it. We have only gradually become aware of the hook in Jesus' promise, "I will be with you all days, even to the end of the world." This not only means he will not go away but that we cannot get rid of him. He continues to roll back the stone from the caves we entomb him in. It is only because Jesus insists on inserting himself into the thick of our plots that we insist on commenting on him.

Part of every preface should be a warning to the reader. This book is written by a Church person for Church people. This does not mean the parchments of orthodoxy are unrolled and the towering sentences of Nicea and Chalcedon solemnly read. The term "Church person" is not meant to be derogatory. Often, in the Puritan imagination of

the counter-culture, the Church person is pictured
as an obligation-hounded, money-oriented
hypocrite whose expression of faith ranges from
bingo to the parish picnic. But the average Church
person is well aware that he is tied to both God and
Neighbor and wants to do right by them. He has
inherited a tradition of outlooks and values which
are inspired by the person of Jesus. In this minimal
sense Jesus has always been part of his language
and consciousness. Jesus was one of the gifts he
received from the people who cared about him.
Now the Church person must be about the
maturing business of personally appropriating
him, of finding out who Jesus is and what he means
to his increasingly complex life.

This is a book of religious exploration which has
plundered theological sources for support and
direction. Although scholarship has been
employed, it is not a scholarly work. Although in
places it summarizes, it is not a popular summary.
It is a book about looking through Jesus into the
Mystery we share with him. Its presupposition is
that words about Jesus are self-involving. We do
not dispassionately chat about him and then go our
various ways. To talk about Jesus is to reveal the
nature and depth of our own investment in the
human adventure. In short, this book is a stab at a
Jesus-spirituality.

Every book has an ambition which hopes too
much. In this case it is the attempt to find a middle
road between unfeeling theological dissections of
Christ and mindless allegiance to a fundamentalist
Jesus. On the one hand, religious explorations of

Jesus must not translate him into esoteric language: Since Jesus belongs to all humankind, any understanding of him must fight against exclusivism. Yet the Jesus who has suffered extensively under the theological scalpel seldom recovers his power to enthrall and motivate human life. The only access to him becomes a metaphysical maze which few can travel. On the other hand, there must be a Jesus other than the one who miraculously saves Mickey Rooney from drugs: there must be a way of loyalty to Jesus which does not mean disloyalty to the fullness of contemporary concerns and knowledge. The brittle and unyielding Jesus of fundamentalism generates Bible-thumping righteousness and a pushy certitude which protests too much. It is a style which does not recognize complexity and confronts every situation with platitude. A faith response to Jesus can never mean abandoning reason. Faith is an eyes-open movement into Mystery and not an eyes-shut, hard swallow of the incredible. Between theological aridity and fundamentalist simplism is the road which (hopefully) the challenging Jesus walks.

Besides warning readers, a preface should thank friends and helpers. This book would never have been shaped into correctly spelled words and readable sentences without the patience and cooperation of Mrs. Rita Troccoli and her magic typewriter.

Chapter I

What Think Ye Of The Christs?

> Later he saw Jesus move from tree to tree in the
> back of his mind, a wild ragged figure
> motioning him to turn around and come off
> into the dark where he was not sure of his
> footing, where he might be walking on water
> and not know it and then suddenly know it
> and drown.[1]
>
> — Flannery O'Connor

Jesus not only stalks the fevered brain of Hazel
Motes, the backwoods prophet of Flannery
O'Connor's *Wise Blood*, but the psyche of the
Western person. He moves from generation to
generation, sometimes reviled and sometimes
prayed to, sometimes the center of controversy and
sometimes mere religious tinsel, sometimes a
ragged figure motioning from the darkness and
sometimes the splendiferous Pantocrator gloriously
reigning—but he is always there. Jesus is a cultural
constant, one of those ineluctable societal facts
which everybody at one time or another must
confront. In another of Flannery O'Connor's
stories, *Parker's Back*, Obadiah Elihu Parker has a
stern Byzantine Christ tatooed on his back. He
hoped it would please his shrewish, religious wife
but discovers that "the all-demanding eyes" of the

15

Christ want him. Jesus not only haunts the psyche of the Western person but is burned into the flesh. It is undoubtedly true that humankind is entering a new age, a post-Christendom era, but it also seems likely that a persistent and resilient companion of that future will be Jesus.

Contemporary awareness and fascination with Jesus is remarkable when contrasted with the current devaluation of God and Church. A standard cultural observation is that God (whoever or whatever that name may refer to) no longer commands time and attention. He cannot compete with technological man who answers petitions for health and rain with wonder drugs and cloud seeding and not with mysterious silence which theologians struggle to interpret as communication. Autonomous humankind, although neither all-powerful nor all-knowing, is, within its powers, more responsive. But even those people who prematurely and cavalierly have dug a grave for God do not want an accident to befall Jesus. The contagion of Christ's freedom must be spread. Today's person must live the ethics of Jesus in the world. To borrow biblical imagery, the Father may be eclipsed but the Son remains prominent.

A similar situation prevails with regard to the Church. Within the last fifteen years the most penetrating criticism of Roman Catholicism has been from within. The divine element in the ecclesial make-up, once almost visible to the eyes of the faithful, has been overshadowed by gross power plays intent on the survival of an authoritarian style. The warts on the Bride of Christ have never been so obvious to so many people. Yet in the face of this sustained and rigorous criticism, the founder has remained unscathed. In fact, it is not only that Jesus has been spared the venom but that often the ecclesiastical critiques have been launched in his name. Jesus is called upon to purge the Church and the Church to realign herself under his Lordship. Many contemporary attacks on the Church end with the sigh, "Fortunately, Christ is greater than the Church."[2] Of course no true understanding of Jesus can separate him from his Father or the community founded in his name. But the emphasis is significant. In our day the reentry into the Sacred and the restructuring of the Church may well come through a renewed understanding of the challenge of Jesus.

The fact that in our culture Jesus is unavoidable also makes unavoidable the question put to Peter at Caesarea Philippi, "Who do you say that I am?" and later classically formulated as "What think ye of the Christ?" But today the only honest answer, in the great tradition of Jewish debate, would be another question—which Christ? This is not a matter of mysticism. Which Christ does not refer to Gerard Manley Hopkins' Christ who plays in ten-thousand places or the Lord who resides in the least of his brethren and is suddenly discovered in J. D. Salinger's breakthrough sentence, "Buddy, the fat lady is Jesus Christ." The multiple Jesuses which abound in our time are various renderings of the historical Jesus. A recent cartoon portrays this quandary about the many Christs. It takes off from the now-defunct television game show *To Tell The*

Truth. Three contestants claim to be the same person, e.g. Fred Talmidge, and then each tries to persuade a panel that he is the real Fred. The cartoon pictures three Christs: the Christ of Protestant piety, a haloed and radiant gentle-teacher; the Christ of Catholic piety, long-faced with sorrow and crowned with thorns; the third Christ, an obviously haggard, certainly disgusted, militantly Jewish, middle-aged man. The caption reads, "Will the real Jesus please stand up?" Within today's debunking mood there is no doubt which cartoon figure will stand up. Traditional Protestant and Catholic spirituality have manhandled Jesus, albeit unknowingly, into a teacher of whimpering love and a melancholic man who silently endures the lash. But these two images no longer have automatic priority for understanding Jesus. They must enter the marketplace and compete with myriad other images which seek to disclose the reality of the person who is Jesus the Christ.

Of the two Jesuses who are presently in vogue, one is a Superstar and the other is under the spell of God. "Jesus Christ Superstar" draws the painful breaths of an existentialist anti-hero. He knows the absurdity of his apostles, the mob, the world, and the demands of God. Nevertheless he grits his teeth, acts, and achieves authenticity by risking his life to his deepest, even though ambigious, impulses. His consciousness is revealed in his garden prayer to God, "Take me before I change my mind." The Jesus of *Godspell* is, in many ways, exactly the opposite. He is a flower-child, a man without guile. He straightens the labyrinthine lies of the mind with simplicity; defuses the alarm system on the heart with openness; breaks down the defenses of the ego with smiles. He is the revelation of the devastating gentleness of God.

The last half of the nineteenth century, under the dizzying effects of the new Scripture criticism, was the age of the biographies of Jesus. The most popular and in many circles most infamous attempt to reconstruct Jesus was Ernst Renan's *The Life of Jesus* (1863). The Jesus of Renan is basically a romantic who falls upon bad days. He begins his ministry under the blue heaven of Galilee, wanders the eternal hills with gentle fisher-folk, and preaches a "delicieuse theologie d'amour." But these golden days soon vanish as gentle teacher turns fanatic, his mind obsessed with apocalyptic terrors. He becomes a charlatan and the raising of Lazarus is portrayed as a publicity stunt to enhance his reputation. In the agony of Gethsemane with his death "near at hand" Jesus' mind turns back to Galilee and the girl he loved. This cloying ending prompted a comment from a young French woman (it is reported), "What a pity it does not end in a marriage."

Marriage, in fact, is the last temptation Jesus faces in the fictional biography by Nikos Kazantzakis. The Christ of Kazantzakis is a hesitant carpenter whom God, portrayed as an eagle, sinks his talons into and flies to destiny. This destiny is his death on the cross which will mysteriously promote the cause of God on earth. His last temptation is to refuse this divine mission, settle down, wed Mary

Magdalene, and from a rocker on his porch watch his grandchildren play in the yard. Jesus is the man who triumphed over domesticity and entrusts his life to a great creative enterprise. *The Last Temptation of Christ* is the reeling account of a man caught between the comforts of this life and his transcendent call. Death is loyalty to his call and release from his torment.

Quite popular in recent years has been a Marxist interpretation of Jesus. Jesus, conscious of the fact that class struggle is the inherent nature of society, led a proletarian revolt. He tried to gather and organize the lowliest of the low—the people of the land, the outcasts, the politically and religiously unclean of Palestine. The more respectable of Jesus' band saw this infatuation with the poor unnecessary and destructive. This tactical disagreement escalated into enmity and Jesus' eventual betrayal and crucifixion. Comrade Jesus can be contrasted to the ludicrous, capitalistic portrayal given by a young and rising financier in Robertson Davies' *Fifth Business:*

> I mean, Christ was really a very distinguished person, a Prince of the House of David, a poet and an intellectual. Of course He was a carpenter; all those Jews in Bible days could do something with their hands. But what kind of a carpenter was He? Not making cowsheds, I'll bet. Undoubtedly a designer and a manufacturer, in terms of those days. Otherwise, how did He make his connections? You know, when He was travelling

around, staying with all kinds of rich and
influential people as an honored guest—obviously
He wasn't just bumming his way through
Palestine; He was staying with people who knew
Him as a man of substance who also had a great
philosophy. You know, the way those Orientals
make their pile before they go in for philosophy.
And look how He appreciated beauty! When that
woman poured the ointment on His feet, He knew
good ointment from bad, you can bet. And the
Marriage at Cana—a party, and He helped the host
out of a tight place when the drinks gave out,
because He had probably been in the same fix
Himself in His days in business and knew what
social embarrassment was. And an economist!
Driving the money-changers out of the
Temple—why? Because they were soaking the
pilgrims extortionate rates, that's why, and
endangering a very necessary tourist attraction and
rocking the economic boat. It was a kind of market
discipline, if you want to look at it that way, and he
was the only one with the brains to see it and the
guts to do something about it . . . that may have
been at the back of the Crucifixion; the priests got
their squeeze out of the Temple exchange, you can
bet, and they decided they would have to get rid of
this fellow who was possessed of a wider economic
vision.[3]

Perhaps the most popular image of Jesus,
especially within the Churches is that of the
heavenly visitor. This image is the enduring
foundation of gnostic and Docetic tendencies. Jesus
is the pre-existent Son of God who is sent on a
mission of redemption by the Father. He not only
knows what is in man but future is ancient history

to him. He is the only actor in the human drama who has the entire script. He touches upon earth, walks through his role, and springs heavenward. Jesus is the God who came to dinner. His suffering and death were a good show but at the first crack of the whip he retreated within himself to the Beatific Vision. In one version the God-Jesus does not really die. In the second, before expiration, he escapes the disposable body and flies home. The divinity of this Jesus completely overshadows and eventually swallows his humanity. This image of Jesus reached a modernized logical extreme a few years back when someone marshalled an airtight (sic) argument proving that Jesus was an astronaut from another planet.

Given the current romance with revolution it is not surprising that a Jesus would appear who looks remarkably like Che Guevara. Jesus, it seems, was a Zealot. The Zealots were the organized resistance movement of the Jews against the Roman occupation. Jesus' crime is not a pretention to divinity but an actual grab for political power. He is crucified for sedition. The leitmotif of his preaching is, "I have come not to bring peace but division."[4] and his first commandment, "If you have no sword, sell your cloak and buy one."[5] Under the influence of the peace movement this violent Jesus gives way to a pacifist. Although Jesus is born into a violent world (the slaughter of the innocents) and violently taken from it, he does not respond in kind. He is a sheep beneath the shears and admonishes that those who use the sword shall perish by it.[6] He rebukes Peter and James who want to send fire from heaven (ala Elijah) on the friendly Samaritan village and rejects a violent interpretation of the Messiah. Add to this a turned cheek and unresisted evil and the image of a pacifist Jesus emerges.

Hugh Schonfield's *The Passover Plot* insists that Jesus be interpreted in Jewish categories, most notably that of the Messiah. Jesus believed himself to be the Expected One of Israel and the way to prove messiahship was to fulfill the prophesies of the Scriptures. So Jesus went about not doing good but scheming and plotting how to fulfill Isaiah here, and bring Ezekiel to fruition there. One of the prophecies Jesus sought to fulfill was that the Messiah should suffer, but not perish, on the cross. So he rigged up a crucifixion and planned to take a drug which would give the appearance of death. Joseph of Arimathea would then quickly take his body to his own private tomb and revive him. Unfortunately the unforseen thrust of a Roman lance rendered the clever Jesus not a messianic pretender but (to stay within Jewish categories) a schlemiel. The trickster had been out-tricked.

Harvey Cox believes the image of Christ as a harlequin can have redemptive power for modern humankind. In a world which doublethinks its fun, Christ brings a true sense of festivity. Harvey Cox finds the biblical picture of Christ crowded with clown symbols. "Like the jester, Christ defies custom and scorns crowned heads. Like a wandering troubadour he has no place to lay his head. Like the clown in the circus parade, he satirizes existing authority by riding into town replete with regal pageantry when he has no earthly power. Like a minstrel he frequents dinners and parties. At the end he is costumed by his enemies in a mocking caricature of royal paraphernalia. He is crucified amidst sniggers and taunts with a sign over his head that lampoons his laughable claim."[7]

"One way!" they shout when you meet them and that way is Christ. They are the Jesus freaks. They have all the sociological signs of a craze and by the time this comment is in print will probably have gone the way of the hulahoop. Yet they have a distinctive image of Jesus as a Big Brother Superego. Jesus is the one who tells them they can kick the drug habit and gives them the strength to do it. Jesus is the friend who readily forgives and forgets the past but demands you shape up in the future. The most recent plundering of Christian mythology is Jonathan Livingston Seagull Christ. Undoubtedly he will prove the highest flying, shortest-lived Christ of them all. Richard Bach would have us believe that Jesus grunted his way to divinity, the little seagull that could. In the Middle Ages a symbol for Christ was the phoenix, that mythical bird which rose from its ashes. In our own time the mating of the work ethic and aeronautics has given birth to Jonathan Livingston Seagull Christ.

The permutations of Jesus seem endless. Adolf Holl (*Jesus in Bad Company*) wants to interpret Jesus sociologically as a criminal whose deviate behavior threatened the good order of society. Cleage envisions a Black Messiah who came to teach black folk how to fight white folk. In one opinion Jesus was a feminist ultimately concerned about

women's liberation; in another, Jesus is a homo-
sexual proclaiming a bizzare understanding of
brotherly love and a new sexual ethic. One of the
latest discoveries has Jesus a magician engaging in
libertine nocturnal rituals. And on and on and on.
The plastic face of Jesus is pulled into a smile or a
scowl; his eyes are angry or ecstatic; his words are
comfort or death. But amid the myriad Christs some
prize must be given to John Allegro for his ultimate
transformation of Jesus into a hallucinogenic mush-
room.

The many images of Jesus are meant to be
complimentary. They affirm Jesus' status as a
culture hero. His endorsement of every cause and
philosophical position is eagerly sought after. Jesus
brings instant authority and a sense of moral
imperative. If Jesus is for Women's Lib, who can be
against it? The mistake many Church people make
is to view the images of Jesus as the carefully
planned ridicule of the Divine Son of God by people
of ill-will. This is hardly the case. Each and every
Jesus is an attempt to portray the authentic man
according to a certain vision of life. For example, the
point of Superstar is not that there is no resurrection
as so many orthodox Christians notice. The point is
that in an ambiguous world Jesus risks his life and
acts authentically. Superstar may lack the fullness of
the Gospel portrayal but it is not malicious. Its
purpose is not to slur Christian faith but to speak it
in contemporary accents. In these images Christ
becomes, to use Jung's phrase, "the ideal of the
self," an inkblot in which each person sees what he
considers true manhood. The many images of Jesus

even when they most offend traditional Christian sensibilities, as with D. H. Lawrence's reduction of the resurrection to sexual awareness, are stumbling attempts to compliment Jesus of Nazareth.

Unfortunately the many images of Jesus go beyond compliment into propaganda. With the advent of mass communication every social organization from national government to advertising agency has become skilled in the art of propaganda. Propaganda is more than just a slanted view on things. It is news given with the ulterior motivation of enlisting the listener for the purposes of the propagandist. It is a complex and subtle form of manipulation which is at its best when it is not noticed. Propaganda is not necessarily lies but the skillful selection of facts to promote a certain goal. For our purposes, two elements of propaganda must be clearly seen. First, the propagandist is concerned with the listener only insofar as he promotes the government, corporation, or ideology, etc. of the propagandist. The listener himself is of no use except as a person to be enlisted. Second, propaganda always uses the presuppositions of its hearers but never challenges them. Leander Keck points out how Christian preaching can suddenly be transformed into propaganda. "Christian preaching becomes propaganda when it adopts the current ideology instead of entering into a struggle with it. It becomes propaganda when current myths and assumptions control what is said or not said, whether it be 'religious individualism' as the sacred counterpart to 'the free enterprise system' (*Christian economics*), or religious zealotism as the hand-maiden of radical reconstruction."[8]

Many images of Jesus qualify as propaganda. Jesus becomes the unwitting embodiment of the fashionable ideology. He is reduced to what in his lifetime he vehemently resisted—a seller of ideas. In this guise he is never good news to the hearer but only a promotion gimmick. Jesus—whether with a crown of thorns on his head or a lily in his hand or a machine-gun on his shoulder—is a recruitment poster. His outstretched finger is accosting passers-by: "Existentialism, hippyism, revolution wants you!"

Many people in the Church want to avoid this propagandizing of Jesus by avoiding images. Only one image of Jesus is legitimate and for the Catholic that image is the God-Man, one person and two natures formulated at Chalcedon.[9] No other image will even be considered. This opinion does not recognize that the power and mystery of the person of Jesus generates many images even within the New Testament. Multiple images, although prone to propaganda, are also a sign of vitality. The story of Jesus, his call and temptations, his preaching and mission, his death and resurrection are so engrained in the Western psyche that it continues to fascinate and call forth ever-new variations. Also, to attempt an exhaustive appraisal of Jesus in a single image subtly undermines the richness of divine activity connected with his life. Jesus lives out of a transcendence which first reduces humankind to wondering silence and then to a riot of metaphors. Images explore this mystery of Jesus.

but in no way exhaust it. Further, Jesus-imaging is the way Western people ask the meaning of life. The many Jesuses are personal and collective searches for a cause to be committed to, a passion to be consumed by, a life which has worth and purpose. Explorations into Jesus are not only historical expeditions but the way the self asks its deepest questions.

What is needed amid this flurry of Jesuses is a controlling perspective. There must be an angle of vision which can gather in what is consonant with the Jesus tradition and exclude what is dissonant. The Christian seeks this perspective in the New Testament. This in itself is a perilous task which the next chapter will explore. But if there is no controlling image, the many Jesuses merely become splattered confusions. The tradition is flippantly tampered with and the person and symbol of Jesus the Christ is drained of impact and persuasion. The many Jesuses, not grounded and critiqued by Jesus the Christ of the New Testament, appear playthings, darlings of current concern, usable and disposable figures. They do not carry life or death significance; allegiance to them is not a matter of redemption but of preference. The real danger of the many Jesuses is that they transform Jesus from a two-edged sword into a curiosity piece. In the history of Western Christianity Jesus has been discounted and pushed to the side for many reasons. Today the ultimate discrediting of Jesus is that since nobody knows his name, anybody can call him anything.

Chapter 2

Jesus As Challenge

The quandary of the many Jesuses looks to the Gospels for direction. The hope is that in these foundational Christian documents a Jesus with sharp features and ringing voice will stand up and claim Christhood. The imposters and half-Jesuses will be exposed as pretenders. Their falseness, inadequacy, and even deceitfulness will be obvious to all. Many Catholics might wish to make the Chalcedonian Christ with his orthodox psyche of one person and two natures the touchstone Jesus. But most Catholics would admit that the carefully chiseled Christ of Catholic dogma is the Gospel Jesus unpacked and appropriately thought through. So the Christian turns past Church Councils to the source work of Christianity. With simple enough logic he looks to the original Jesus to critique the latecomers. Yet the Gospels are a surprising place to look, for in the last hundred and fifty years they have been the problem not the solution.

The unabashed fact is that the Gospels are not what contemporary sensibilities want them to be. They do not reflect the dominant mood of American culture. A cultural mood is a thinking and feeling

29

climate which establishes what will be taken for granted and what will not be taken at all. It is comprised of presuppositions which, although rarely alluded to in themselves, enter into and shape the general consciousness. This mood develops when one aspect of the human endeavor, usually one which is successful and finds ready acceptance, is escalated into a world-view. A limited way of dealing with a certain area of reality becomes the norm by which all of life is judged and validated. The mood which until recently has characterized American life might be labeled scientism. This mood takes as axiomatic that whatever exists can be sensibly detected and that the way of truth is detached, impartial observation. Although many philosophers of science are trying to correct this overly positivistic emphasis, it is still the assumed cultural criterion of what is real.

Historians, especially under the influence of Von Ranke, have attempted to adopt this scientific model. The rigorous but narrow method which has made the natural sciences so successful is transferred to historical data. The unimpeachable source becomes the uninvolved copier of facts. What must be searched out are the writings of those neutral people with no axes to grind. The archivist becomes the bedrock of historical science. Although this stance greatly tightens a loose and gullible acceptance of historical documents, it tends to overlook that history is made and recorded by free human beings and therefore less predictable than observations of "natural laws." Grunt as one might, a social science cannot be transformed into a physical one. Nevertheless, this scientific mood makes us feel uneasy with historical probability and increases our lust for certitude. That magic word "objectivity" which is often stringently defined as the elimination of all human fingerprints, is what we feel we need before we can give credence. We want historical reports to have the same clarity and exactitude as a chemical compound. So when the Christian turns to the Gospels to find the real Jesus, he expects a neutral, journalistic rendering and becomes dismayed when it is explained that everything is smudged by faith. It is no accident that many people turn to Jim Bishop's *The Day Christ Died* with its fictional accuracy and pinpoint detail to explain their Jesus to them. In short the Gospels are expected to play Boswell to Jesus' Dr. Johnson and the disconcerting fact is that they do not.

The Gospels are the experiences of Jesus played upon the blue guitar.

> They said, "You have a blue guitar,
> You do not play things as they are."
> The man replied, "Things as they are
> Are changed upon the blue guitar."
> And they said then, "But play, you must,
> A tune beyond us, yet ourselves,
> A tune upon the blue guitar
> Of things exactly as they are."[1]

The blue guitar is the resurrection faith of the early Church. This faith penetrates the mystery of the historical Jesus and shapes the Gospel stories. Jesus is never considered apart from this responding faith in him. His story is always played upon the blue guitar which knows he is "a tune beyond us, yet ourselves" and that things exactly as they are are always more than they appear to be. The resurrection experience turns the conundrum of Jesus' life and death into the mystery of God's redemptive act. It is the risen Christ who interprets the meaning of the historical Jesus. In this way the Gospels do not end with the resurrection but begin with it. The last chapter was written first and it dictated the middle and the beginning. Bruce Vawter states it well. "It began with the resurrection. Perhaps it were better said, it had begun long before, but with the resurrection began understanding."[2] The Gospels then are not mirrors held up to Jesus but faith responses to him.

To understand the development of the Gospels—the early Church's appropriation and response to the life, death, and resurrection of Jesus—the perspectives of form and redaction criticism are helpful. Form criticism is keenly aware that the sayings and stories of the Gospels were orginally independent units transmitted orally within the Christian community. The history of this transmission and the changes the material underwent is what form criticism investigates. Certain stories were remembered because they served the catechetical, missionary, liturgical, or disciplinary needs of the community. A form critic asks the question: "Was the story of Jesus and his disciples eating corn on the Sabbath recalled for polemical use against the Sabbath regulations of mainstream Judaism?" Other stories were embellished and tidied up as the Church developed certain theological convictions. For example, in Mark's version of Jesus' visit to his home town Jesus could do no mighty work there: ". . . and he could work no miracle there, though he cured a few sick people by laying his hands on them. He was amazed at their lack of faith."[3] In Matthew this is stated quite differently: ". . . and he did not work many miracles there because of their lack of faith."[4] Two changes have occurred. The "could not" of Mark which denotes power in bondage changes to a "did not" in Matthew which is merely a neutral statement that nothing happened. Also Jesus' surprise at the failure of his townfolk to respond is omitted in Matthew. Did the image of Jesus as all-powerful and all-knowing develop to such an extent that Matthew thought it was inconsistent that he be powerless and ignorant? The perduring question for form criticism is: "Did the community create stories about Jesus which did not have an actual historical reference? Did the blue guitar create music of its own or did it resonate and explore the sound of Jesus?" No global answer can be given to that question. Each individual segment must be considered in itself. For example, most scholars feel the story of Peter walking on the water is a creation of the Christian community. It was meant to illustrate the early Church's dependence on Jesus for the continuation of life. But the baptism narrative, no matter how elaborated, is indisputably based on an incident in the life of Jesus. Our purpose is not to unravel the highly sophisticated methodology of form criticism but to underline the ineluctable fact that the datum of the Gospels is not Jesus but Jesus and the early Church.

If form criticism deals with the oral transmission of individual Gospel material, redaction criticism is concerned with the contribution of the evangelist, the person who put it all together. The actual arrangement and editing of stories within the Gospels are not haphazard bunching but usually reveal a theological purpose. One of the best examples of redaction criticism is Hans Conzelmann's *The Theology of St. Luke.* It was commonly thought that Luke shared the contemporary obsession with dates and places. His interests were historical and so, unlike John, he could be counted on to get things straight. For example, Luke places the post-resurrection experiences of Jesus in Jerusalem and not, as the other Gospels suggest, in Galilee. But the reason for this according to Conzelmann is not a passion for historical accuracy but to emphasize a theological vision. In Luke's salvation history Jerusalem plays a key role and so the Jesus who died there must also appear there as risen. Luke's Gospel is a response to the early Church's most urgent theological question: "Why has Jesus not come back?" Luke's answer (which is more of a vision) is a three-stage salvation history which would be repeated and expanded throughout Christian history. The first stage is from Israel to John the Baptist; the second is the ministry of Jesus which is the center of time; the third is the period of the Church which looks backward to the historical Jesus and forward to his Second Coming. The important emphasis is that the Age of the Church may not be a brief interlude but an indefinite extension of time. Luke's is the Gospel that understands that the Church must, to some extent, settle into history and come to terms with time. Redaction criticism, like form criticism, brings the awareness that the Gospels are not examples of modern historiography but texts which document the ongoing experience of the early Church whose historic and symbolic center was Jesus.

This development of the Gospels and so of the Jesus who dwells within them is concretely suggested in Luke's story of the Road to Emmaus. The two disillusioned disciples represent the early community. The journey did not take an afternoon but a few generations and, in a very real way, continues today. The disciples know the facts of Jesus' life and death and even are aware of resurrection reports; but they do not understand their meaning. In their dialogue with each other and in the burning understanding of the Scriptures which the stranger gives them the meaning of Jesus begins to break through. "Did not the Messiah have to suffer these things in order to enter into his glory?"[5] In their common meal, the ancient rite which symbolizes the fellowship of humankind, the stranger is revealed as Jesus the Christ. This story eloquently tells how the early Church gradually appropriated the meaning of its Lord—by interpreting him through the Scriptures and by sharing the common meal in his memory and in the hope of his return. Jesus the Christ is the result of a long process of meditating on Scriptures and experiencing him in the community gathered in his name. The Gospels do not give us a fleeting and scarcely understood stranger but a pondered-over and lived-with Lord.

The highly complex nature of the Gospels (which has only been hinted at here) does not mean that the historical Jesus (that Jesus who is recoverable by modern historiography) is beyond reach. In the past this was often thought to be the case. What developed was a defensive Christology which claimed the results of historical research had nothing to do with Christian faith. The argument was that faith could not be based on the fluctuations of historical judgment. Extreme and shocking statements were made: "Even if historians eventually conclude that Jesus never existed, Christian faith would be valid." What was salvific was the Christ of faith who was encountered in the Preached Word within the ecclesial community. Whether this Christ of faith had actual roots in the lived existence of Jesus of Nazareth was a matter of interest to the ancient historian but not to the believer. This way of thinking both stresses and neglects an important truth. The stressed truth is that historical facts about Jesus, as historical facts (age, height, marital status), are not salvific. Only the Jesus responded to in faith redeems life. The neglected truth is that if the preached Christ is not inspired and informed by the concrete historical person of Jesus of Nazareth, we have a floating myth, a Christ spun from enthusiasm and fantasy who inhabits the heavens of the imagination. But what we know is needed is that one of us, a sharer in this existence we call human, lived life in such a way that contact with him is redemptive.

The fact that the Gospels indiscriminately mix faith, history, and theology should not panic us into thinking Jesus is fictional. It only means that it will take sophisticated prosecution for the faith-saturated Gospels to yield the historical data about Jesus which the contemporary mood values. Perhaps the best set of categories for fielding the complexities of the Gospels has been proposed by Van Harvey.[6] He distinguishes four meanings to the phrase Jesus of Nazareth. The first is the actual past person who lived and died. This person like all past people is not fully recoverable. The second is the historical Jesus. This is the Jesus who is now recoverable through the methods of modern historiography. Harvey succinctly states that he is what "can be fairly said about the actual Jesus on the basis of our inferences from our present sources."[7] The third Jesus is constituted by the memory impression of the early Church. This Jesus is highly selective. He was remembered for a particular reason, cherished because he answered a certain need. "This image is not unlike a bas-relief in which everything irrelevant from the standpoint of those who preserved it was carefully chiseled away."[8] The fourth meaning of Jesus of Nazareth is the Biblical Christ. By this Harvey means the transformation of the memory impression of Jesus under the influence of theological interpretation. The Johannine Jesus, the preexistent Word of God come down from heaven, is a good example of the Biblical Christ. These various Jesuses should not

surprise us. All ancient historical documents
require the same nuanced approach and careful
handling.

In the movement from the actual Jesus to the
Biblical Christ there is obvious discontinuity.
These two Jesuses often look and act like two
different people. What must be insisted on is that
this surface discontinuity masks a deeper
continuity. From the historical Jesus to the Biblical
Christ is not a giant, unwarranted leap but the
gradual unfolding of the meaning of Jesus. The
Biblical Christ is not community effervescence but a
community response to the mystery they
encountered (more precisely the mystery which
grasped them). All that was Jesus' life, death, and
resurrection demanded time in which to be
assimilated and images in which to be expressed.
The unpacking of Jesus by the early Church,
especially in the bestowing of titles, is neither
arbitrary tampering nor betrayal of his raw
humanity but fidelity to what came to expression in
him. An emphasis on the legitimacy of the Biblical
Christ is not a putdown of the search for the
historical Jesus. The delineation of the historical
Jesus is the foremost apologetic task which
respects, as it should, the historical consciousness
of ourselves and our culture. Not to ground Jesus
historically is to retreat from credibility into a
privately owned knowledge which does not
dialogue with the dominant cultural spirit. Such a
haughty retreat might have worked in the citadel
Church but in a community which values open
lines of communication it would be a fearful and
suspect move.

The danger is that in the rush to establish the historicity of Jesus the symbols which the early Church used to explore his mystery will be discarded. These symbols are definitely culture bound, as historically dated as tentmaking. They cannot be spoken directly but need mountains of interpretation to release their power and meaning. Yet for all their archaism they are the first-formed language of faith. It is what people said after Jesus entered their lives. To see in the Church's struggling symbolic affirmation of Jesus only old words would be to misunderstand the joyous and desperate imperative of faith. Faith must bring to language what is experienced in and through Jesus yet it knows all words will fail. For all its conviction, faith has a mystic side which realizes orthodoxy is not adequacy but merely the least harmful betrayal of God. In its search for expression, faith ransacks all cultural forms. Everything is pressed into service and juggled before the experienced Reality. When faith frolics, and that seems to be what it does best, it creates images. This symbol-making is not out to make a laborious point but for sheer delight the mind somersaults on the high wire. Faith gazes into the kaleidoscope of God, Humankind, Christ, History, and Nature and is lost in the beautiful mix. The symbols of faith are the result of the Child of Wisdom playing among the stars. Therefore we do not abandon the Biblical Christ with his ancient theological trappings but reverence him as faith's response to the historical Jesus. The ancient symbols are more than attic material kept out of fondness or nostalgia. They are the symbolic entrance into the Reality which Jesus disclosed and in which, we, as Christians, scandalously dwell as we thrash about in the present and fashion a usable future.

The emphasis on the historical Jesus anchors us in space and time and not solely in the mind of humankind. The awareness and treasuring of the Biblical Christ reminds us that the Gospels contain a faith-response and are places of encounter. Also, the historical Jesus and the Biblical Christ, although not facsimiles, are not strangers. The exact extent and nature of the overlap and continuity is the sophisticated and painstaking work of biblical scholarship. But there is one sweeping similarity which provides a significant focus on the event of Jesus the Christ. The style of the historical Jesus which is also reflected, however dimly, in the Biblical Christ is challenge-invitation. Jesus' presence, and the later faith proclamation of his life, confronts presuppositions and life styles. But this confrontation does not take sledgehammer delight in shattering the well-wrought world of its hearer. At the heart of the challenge is an invitation to newness, a call to restructure what has so suddenly been dismantled. The area of challenge-invitation is the enduring triad of God, self, and neighbor. This is to say in more philosophical language that Jesus the Christ uncovers the dialectical relationship between religious conviction and ethical behavior. This is the area, the area of ultimacy and its ethical implications, which Jesus stakes out and which the early Church concentrates on in proclaiming its faith in him.

The challenge-invitation style of the historical Jesus is clearly seen in the parables. Most scholars agree that the parables in their tone and meaning are creations of Jesus. The early church would often alter a parable into an allegory (e.g. the sower and the seed) or an exemplary story (e.g. the ending of the Good Samaritan, "Go and do likewise," is Luke's addition). But the original parabolic form is distinct in itself and meant to be taken as a whole. It had only one point to make and, like a joke, we either get it or we don't. This singleness of purpose of the parable means that it does not call forth intellectual questions or labored discussions but flashing insights and decisions. Parables are not stated conclusions about the Kingdom of God or admonitions to proper behavior. The parable attempts, often by shock, to catapult the hearer into the experience of God. It is never an end in itself but a path to experiencing aspects of the Kingly activity of God—forgiveness, human solidarity, repentance, hope, etc. The parable is not a Great Truth to be looked at and admired but a glass of vision to be looked through. In this way, parables are not teachings but invitations to participate in the religious reality which consumes Jesus and which is revealed in him. In John Dominic Crossan's phrase, echoing Heidegger, "Parable is the house of God."[9]

What must be emphasized is the relationship of the parable to freedom. Most forms of teaching, even those which claim to be non-directive, subtly coerce. There is always a guru who, with superior knowledge or exceptional skill in relating, cajoles his hearers along a predetermined path. With Jesus the parable is spoken and we are left to decision. There is no browbeating, no appeal to higher knowledge, no threat heaped upon threat until a bowed and beaten response is given. The power of the parable is its ability to reveal the hidden dimension of our lives and the possibilities for our future. It authenticates itself by displaying the truth of who we are and what we must be about. In this way it remains a challenge and an invitation to human freedom but no more than that. Some of those who heard the parables thought Jesus was talking about someone else. Others knew the words were addressed to them but they would not risk their lives in order to gain them. Still others generously dwelled within the parables and became children of the Kingdom. The parable allows a wide range of responses but does not force any.

Leander Keck has best captured this challenge-invitation style of Jesus by naming him the "Parable of God."[10] Jesus not only tells stories which challenge accepted views and call for new understanding and action but his very presence and the series of events which constitute his life are parabolic. Like the parable, Jesus did not attract attention to himself but insisted people encounter the Reality he proclaimed. He was not impressed with his importance or a seeker after fame but was the human dwelling place where forgiveness and new life could be experienced. The importance of this style for understanding Jesus and Christian life cannot be overestimated. What is valued is not the repetition of ritual or unflinching consistency but transparency to the Father. In and through Jesus, God's Kingly activity is experienced; and if responded to, humankind is empowered to live together in a new way. Jesus is the free and powerful solicitation of human freedom, the entrance into the depths of human life, the Parable of God.

The challenge-invitation style of Jesus is not only evident in the parables but in almost all the Gospel stories. The Johannine version of the call of the first two disciples is a simple and direct example. "On the following day as John stood there again with two of his disciples, Jesus passed, and John stared hard at him and said, 'Look, there is the lamb of God'. Hearing this, the two disciples followed Jesus. Jesus turned round, saw them following and said, 'What do you want?' They answered, 'Rabbi,' -which means Teacher - where do you live?" Come and see' he replied; so they went and saw where he lived, and stayed with him the rest of that day."[11] "Come and see" is Jesus' call, whether explicitly stated or not, to everyone he encounters. A young man comes to Jesus to ask humankind's perennial question, "What must I do to gain eternal life?" Like most young men he is wide-eyed and generous. Also, like most young men, his gods have not had time to form. Jesus says, "You know the commandments." "All these I have kept from my youth," he protests. How far back is the youth of a young man? For him it seems immeasurable but to older people it is only the distance of a smile. The challenge is sudden: All right, I will tell you. You are asking the wrong question. The question is not,

"How do I gain eternal life" but "How do I serve God and humankind?" Eternal life is a gift which is not sought after but responded to. "Sell what you have and come follow me." At this invitation of Jesus the young man grew old and his rich god came to claim him. Whether accepted (as with Andrew and the other disciple) or refused (as with the young man) the challenge and invitation of Jesus is always present.

This style of encounter is central to Jesus and must figure prominently in any Christology. The Christology of the early Church, crystallized in the theological statements of Chalcedon, legitimately and beautifully expounded the mystery of Jesus as the divine Son of God who took on a human nature. Yet in our day this formulation has had the unfortunate side-effect of obscuring the challenge character of Jesus. Jesus as the Son of God takes on the air of a celebrity and his style becomes authoritative. He is followed not because he has radically encountered and broken open human existence but because he had brought "the word from on high." His message is validated because of his genes—his Father is God—and not because he is the deepest truth about us. Entitling Jesus "the Son of God" may be a valid statement of faith but it can also be a deadly act of king-making. In John's Gospel, Jesus escapes the crowd who wish to make him king and flees to the mountains alone. Will we now, when he cannot stop us, crown him? The bestowal of kingship is the highest form of admiration and the subtlest form of avoidance. As a king he can rule over us and we can play the role we play so well—unruly subjects. As king he will issue decrees and decry infractions and not spin stories which sneak past our defenses and remain too long in our consciences. We will make Jesus into everything possible so as not to face the one thing he is—God's challenge and invitation. In every naming of Jesus there lurks the danger that he becomes not the challenge of God who demands free response but the divine hero who rescues us.

The metaphor to use for this process which has happened to Jesus is hardening. The fluid Jesus who flowed into both God and humankind has gradually hardened into a self-contained mold. In a very real sense rigor mortis has set in. The ultimate perversion of Jesus is that he can now be considered without God being revealed or humankind being grasped. Jesus has achieved independent status, status which the parable giver would reject as a hindrance. In this context Jesus becomes a divine fact to be taken into account rather than a revelation to be encountered. As a fact, even a wonderful fact, he remains information and can be approached with the one attitude his contemporaries could not ever manage toward him—indifference. The metaphysical grounding of Jesus as the Son of God establishes the capacity and logic of redemption at the same time it distances him from us experientially. As one divine person and two natures he is conceptually God and man (although many question the viability of this formulation) but the challenge-invitation character is pushed into the background. The Son of God inspires awe, gratitude, praise, and obeisance but not decision.

What has plagued recent Catholicism is a conceptually concise Son of God who does not entice us into the world of his Father.

This hardening of Jesus is most thoroughly accomplished when we install him in a mythic structure and honor him as hero. The divine hero who is an ideal which we participate in and respond to is a valid stage of religious development. But more often than not the divine hero becomes a substitute. He does for us what we cannot do for ourselves. What are heroes for but to bear the burdens which ordinary people cannot carry? We need an Atlas to support the world for us, a Prometheus to steal the fire for us, a Jesus to defeat Satan for us. As people we invest ourselves in the feats of our heroes and feel vicarious victory and defeat. We tend to cling to heroes in a way reminiscent of the person who called, "Lord, Lord," and did not make it into the Kingdom. Therefore the divine hero is always relevant in the sense that escape from responsibility is always attractive. He becomes our champion; we breathe easier and do not change. The divine hero is undoubtedly an ancient religious myth but it involves more spectating than Jesus seemed to allow. That Jesus was crucified for us does not mean we have been saved from crucifixion; that he bore the sins of humankind does not mean we do not need to repent; that he overcame the world does not mean we can succumb to it. Jesus, the divine hero, evokes our sincerest thanks; Jesus, the divine challenge, evokes responsible action in the world.

To rediscover Jesus as personal challenge we

might explore the saying of the Johannine Christ, "I am the Way, the Truth, and the Life."[12] Although it is highly probable that the historical Jesus never made that statement, it beautifully captures the feelings of those who had experienced Jesus. What he was for them he must once again become for us—not only a person but a pathway. In chapter fourteen of John, Jesus is not the way in the sense of a moral guide or a model of leadership. He is the entrance into the religious reality of the Father, into the depths of the God, self, neighbor relationship. It must be stressed that Jesus is a way into the mystery of human existence and not a way out of current problems. When Jesus is asked to speak directly to economic and socio-political fluctuations, he is immediately discredited. Jesus is our contemporary only in the sense that the need to restructure our mind and heart, to replace ourselves in the God, self, neighbor triad, is always the underlying issue. This is an important distinction for an increasing question is: How can a first-century Jew who never got outside Palestine be the way for a twentieth century cosmopolitan person?

The difference between Jesus and us may be only two thousand earth years but it is cultural light years. No stone is left upon a stone of the constructed religious and social world which he lived in and spoke to. We are vastly different people from those first disciples and, despite Kierkegaard's suggestion, no psychological leap backward is possible. The reality of God which was taken for granted in first century Palestine is today constantly questioned. The contemporary person is forced into paradoxes like the absence of God is his presence. This might be a profound mystical truth but only Simone Weil knows. God, in Huxley's clever phrase, is "beginning to resemble not a ruler, but the last fading smile of a cosmic Cheshire cat."[13] Also our neighbor no longer has the good grace and availability to lay by the side of the road. The personal helping hand has given way to a bureaucratic governmental arm. If the world ever was uncomplicated, it is now hopelessly tangled, a ball of many diverse and unrelated pieces of string. Political treaties, economic systems, and mass communication bring the neighbor close but leave him as frightening and insatiable as ever. The world has so economically overlapped, one person's meat is so obviously another person's poison, that the Christian comes to the sorry question—how does one give a cup of cold water in His Name? And it has been discovered that the self, which is everyone's favorite topic and which is defined in terms of post (post-Freudian, post-Christian, post-industrial), has no bottom. Alexander Pope's aphorism, "The proper study of mankind is man," has succinctly justified unrelenting navel-gazing.

It is only half cynical to say that although humankind never ran that well, the last place to look is under the hood. Unworried about survival, except at crisis moments, we have the luxury to quest after fulfillment. The result is that we know more about why we are unhappy than ever before. "Who am I?" is the constant question and the fear is that when "I get it all together" it might not be much. These faces of God, neighbor, and self, cartooned as they are, are not the ones Jesus stared into. So much that is different shapes us so drastically. Yet, as the oracle says, invoked or not, God is present and still only one of three is neighbor to those in need. The differences are monumental but it is still in the interplay of God, self, and neighbor that the human drama is acted out.

Because of the differences between our times and Jesus' he cannot be for us programs and strategies. Because of the foundational sameness he can be perception and style. The Gospel Jesus does not have helpful hints about institutional racism, world hunger, or international government. The Gospels cannot be plunked down on conference, arbitration, and summit tables with the mindless conviction that the solution has arrived. What the Gospel Jesus proclaims is a perception which is the best grounding for healing and a style which evokes communion and common effort. This is not to relegate the Gospels to second place or even to suggest that their role in the human adventure is ancillary. It is to apply them to the roots, the Listening Place of human existence, the heart from which Jesus said comes both wicked designs and faith, false witness and hope, murder and love. We must reverence Jesus for what he is and not bully him into what he is not. When we make Jesus a brilliant psychologist or a consummate politician, he will not be for us the entry into the religious dimension of human existence. This does not mean that the Gospel Jesus neglects psychological wholeness and is not concerned about political unity but that he comes at these realities from a God orientation. The approach of the Gospel Jesus is distinctive. For Christians to relinquish this approach, because at the moment it is not fashionable or its practical consequences are not immediately measurable, is, quite simply, to lose nerve. Jesus is the way into the Mystery of our common existence and, as such, the Christian is called to "journey" with him.

Jesus is not only a pathway into the mystery of existence but he is the truth about that existence. The type of truth which Jesus is goes beyond accurate information or the flawless accounting of facts. Jesus is the truth in the sense that he uncovers what is hidden, brings to light the last dimension of human existence which so often remains in darkness. Humankind has always intuited an ultimacy which surrounds and permeates human living and which gives it character and direction. This ultimacy alternately fascinates and threatens us. We are eager to explore it yet fearful of its power. In our day there is an ostrich-like, head-in-the-sand, effort to avoid confronting ultimacy. But even when the social construction of reality (secularism) is such that it downplays ultimacy and the influence it has on human behavior, it cannot be excluded. Ultimacy is so fundamental a human experience that to suppress it only assures that it will surface more violently. As long as there is birth and death, there will be a whole in which we participate and an ultimacy to which we are irrevocably linked.

Many people drift into an awareness of the ultimate dimension of existence and its crucial significance for human living. Over the years they become conscious of the More, the Whole, the Encompassing, the Context of all their comings and goings. They ruminate on the stars or the sea and move into the ontological wonder that there is anything at all. But today, drift is not the dominant style. Most people crash into ultimacy. In one intense experience, ultimacy overwhelms them. They are flooded with feelings of peace and joy, of exhilaration and fulfillment, of life purified and renewed. These peak experiences are triggered by almost any stimulus—nature, poetry, sexual love, the birth of a child, religious liturgies. These experiences which tap the transcendent potential of the human personality are avidly sought after and variously interpreted. Although they are not predictable and usually last only a short time, peak experiences are considered to be supremely real and of the utmost importance.

This ultimacy which people both drift and crash into exhibits a profound ambiguity. The nature of this ambiguity is revealed in contrasting the similar yet radically different experiences of John Paul Sartre and Avery Dulles. Both Sartre (through his autobiographical character Roquentin in *Nausea*) and Dulles (in his autobiography *Testimonial to Grace*) are triggered into ultimacy while contemplating a tree. Roquentin is in the park:

> The roots of the chestnut tree were sunk in the ground just under my bench. I couldn't remember it was a root any more. I was sitting, stooping forward, head bowed, alone in front of this black, knotty mass, entirely beastly, which frightened me. The chestnut tree pressed itself against my eyes. Green rust covered it halfway up; the bark,

black and swollen, looked like boiled leather.
Knotty, inert, nameless, it fascinated me, filled my
eyes, brought me back unceasingly to its own
existence. The whole stump gave me the
impression of unwillingness, denying its existence
to lose itself in a frenzied excess. I scraped my heel
against this black root: I wanted to peel off some
bark. For no reason at all, out of defiance, to make
the bare pink appear absurd on the tanned leather:
to play with the absurdity of the world. Suddenly I
knew that every existing thing is born without
reason, prolongs itself out of weakness and dies by
chance. [14]

Dulles is strolling through the woods:

As I wandered aimlessly something impelled me to
look contemplatively at a young tree. On its frail,
supple branches were young buds attending
eagerly the spring which was at hand. While my
eyes rested on them the thought came to me
suddenly with all the strength and novelty of a
revelation, that these little buds with their
innocence and meekness followed a rule, a law of
which I as yet knew nothing. How could it be, I
asked, that this delicate tree sprang up and
developed and that all the enormous complexity of
its cellular operations combined together to make it
grow erectly and bring forth leaves and blossoms?
The answer, the trite answer of the schools, was
new to me: that its actions were ordered to an end
by the only power capable of adapting means to
ends—intelligence—and that the very fact that this
intelligence worked toward an end implied
purposiveness—in other words, a will. As I turned
home that evening, the darkness closing round, I
was conscious that I had discovered something
which would introduce me to a new life. Never,
since the eventful day which I have just described,
have I doubted the existence of an all-good and
omnipotent God. [15]

We may not agree with the oppressive black imagery of Sartre or the teleological argument of Dulles but in juxtaposing their experiences the ambiguity of ultimacy leaps out.

There is an increasing amount of literature on these peak experiences which broaden consciousness to include ultimacy.[16] They are more common than most people think and they enrich rather than impoverish the person. Yet for the religious person a dangerous temptation often accompanies transcendent experiences. When they are exclusively focused on, religion can degenerate into a search for personal highs. The always and everywhere presence and influence of God is overlooked in the quest for transcendent moments. Abraham Maslow goes so far as to equate the future of religion with peakers and non-peakers, those people who have frequent transcendent experiences and those who do not seem capable of them.[17] This emphasis on peak experiences narrows the scope of God's activity considerably and often renders the rest of life religiously unimportant. What must be understood is that religious experience is that moment when the person becomes aware of the religious dimension. The religious dimension is always present and active but only enters consciousness at certain key times. Religious reality is not about "this" experience and "that" experience but about the perduring dimension of ultimacy which grounds and permeates all of human life and which is revealed in "this" experience and "that" experience.

The truth about this ultimacy which appears ambiguous and which, although disclosed in a single experience, is a dimension of existence as revealed in Jesus. What Jesus reveals about ultimate ambiguity and the influence it exerts on human behavior is the thrust of the next five chapters. The present emphasis must be that Jesus is the revelation of our human life and not its proudest exception. That Jesus is not a solitary disclosure, shedding light only on his own special relationship to God and leaving humankind as a whole in the dark, is captured in the ancient *Logos* (Word) Christology. *Logos* was a powerful and controlling concept in both Greek and Hebrew culture. In Greek thought, *Logos* was the divine reason which ordered and sustained the entire universe. It was present everywhere—in the movement of the stars, in the changing of the seasons, in the design of the craftsman, in the processes of the mind. In Hebrew culture *Logos* was the powerful and effective speech of Yahweh. It was present and active at creation. "By the Word of the Lord the heavens were made, their whole array by the breath of his mouth."[18] Isaiah embellishes on the creative powers of God's Word: "Yes, as the rain and the snow come down from the heavens and do not return without watering the earth, making it yield and giving growth to provide seed for the sower and bread for the eating, so the word that goes from my mouth does not return to me empty, without carrying out my will and succeeding in what it was sent to do."[19] Despite their differences these two cultures combine to imagine *Logos* as the universal divine presence which effectively brings about and sustains creation.

In this context, the bold proclamation of the prologue of St. John's Gospel, "The Word has been made flesh," is the announcement of Christian universalism. John is saying that the invisible activity of God throughout creation becomes visible in Jesus. The power and reason which is everywhere present is revealed in this Galilean Jew. Jesus is not a total exception, an unprecedented divine visit; he is total revelation, the uncovering of the hidden but always active God. With this understanding, Jesus is more than just the truth about himself. He is the truth about us insofar as we are related to the ultimate dimension of human existence and to each other. Although John uses the existing cultural concept of *Logos* to explore the mystery of Jesus, he gives it a distinctively Christian turn. The Greeks may have thought of *Logos* as the universal principle of reason but that it would become flesh was repugnant. The Jews knew *Logos* was creative of the world, and even had come to think of Wisdom as personified, but to incarnate the Word in one man at one time and in one place was a daring and shattering move. This is the scandal of particularity—why the God whom heaven and earth cannot contain freely chooses to dwell in the person and life of Jesus of Nazareth. Yet the Christian faith proclaims that this is the case. Jesus the Christ gathers into himself and transforms the general awareness of God. Therefore the Christian drags himself and his encountered ultimacy to Jesus because he knows that there he will meet the truth which will burn away all falseness.

The Jesus who is the Way into, and the Truth about, the mystery of existence, is also Life. Allegiance to Jesus leads us into the religious dimension of God, self, and neighbor and helps us to dwell there truthfully. In truthful dwelling is eternal life. The God-Humankind adventure is too often told from the perspective of how we destroy each other. The Freudian and Marxist critiques of the nineteenth century delighted in detailing how the concept of God drained rather than enhanced the self. In both the personal and social spheres God was a projection which kept humankind from building up its own powers and rectifying social ills. Among humankind there has always been the tension between the biblical notion that we are the keeper of our brothers and sisters and the Latin maxim borne of bitter experience, "Homo homini lupus" (Each person is a wolf to every other). Between God and humankind there is jealous competition, and between the self and the neighbor, barbed wire. We most certainly deal death to each other in swift and violent acts of aggression but we also slowly shrivel because we cease to be rivers of life to each other. Too often we are shrunken people long before breath is gone. The Gospel of John knows this when it insists that alienating sin is the real enemy of life and not physical death. Jesus is Life because he is the Way and Truth by which God, self, and neighbor break their isolation and flow into each other. He is Life because through him God is liberated from the silence of heaven, the self from the imprisonment of the ego, and the neighbor from the role of enemy. Jesus brings God, self, and neighbor together in an everlasting community which is able to withstand the worst that can happen.

With so many contemporary Jesuses claiming Christhood a search through the Gospels seemed the logical way to clear up a case of multiple mistaken identities. We came as decent enough sleuths, magnifying glass in hand, to track down the elusive Jesus. But when we found him, the glass was suddenly turned around and what was enlarged with all its beauty and blemish were our own lives. The afternoon was hot; things were slow; we came to watch the miracles and now we are weighed in the balance. Jesus is no magician but prestidigitation is part of his act. We pursued him out of curiosity and the noble American motive that he might be the greatest man who ever lived. We now push on for a more selfish but also more compelling reason. He is the Way into our thicketed-over lives, the Truth about the ultimacy which is within us and without, the promise of Life which is more than the fast and high thrills of convoluted moments. He has turned on us and touched the enduring zone of existence where God, self, and neighbor interact. It is here that his words are tumblers which open our locked selves and every response, no matter the delicacy of phrasing, is given in terms of cowardice and courage. To understand Jesus as the Founder of the Church or the Eternal Son of God and not realize his very person is a challenge is the difference between prim orthodoxy and discipleship. Jesus wants today what he wanted those long years ago in Palestine—not "heils" from his followers, not the kingdoms of the world for himself, not prayers and sacrifices for his God—but a new heaven and earth; and he seems unable to be dissuaded from the conviction that our free and responsive efforts are what must bring it about. So he is—Yesterday, Today, and the Same Forever—the challenge of God to repent, to celebrate, to trust, to forgive, and to love.

Chapter 3

The Challenge To Repent

Karl Menninger begins his book *Whatever Became of Sin?* with the story of a stern-faced, plainly dressed prophet who haunts the streets of Chicago's Loop. He stands stone-still, solemnly lifts his right arm, singles out one of the passersby, and pronounces the judgment: "Guilty." According to Menninger one of those so accused turned in astonishment to his friend and said, "But how did he know?"[1]

Jesus begins his ministry with the cry, "Repent for the Kingdom of God is near." The opening word of this message confirms John's insight that Jesus knew what was in man.[2] At any moment in history the call to conversion is relevant. The human adventure unfolds East of Eden where Cain kills Abel again and again. Any vision of person and society which does not see its torn and alienated condition is wearing blinders. Despite what Pippa, Browning's innocent little girl, thinks, all is not right with the world. The great American thanksgiving toast, "We have much to be thankful for," is complemented in the honest man by, "We have much to repent for." The words of St. Paul belong to every person, "I fail to carry out the things I want to do, and find myself doing the very things I hate."[3]

No matter what language game is used—religious, psychological, socio-political—the world is convicted of sin. But there is a vast difference between the style of Karl Menninger's street-corner prophet and Jesus. The Chicago prophet is a finger-wagger. His rhetoric may push into the dark corners of our souls and swamp us with guilt but we are left unrepentant. His style appeals to the strange masochism of the psyche which finds no experience so pleasurable as being morally whipped. Wallowing in guilt, an activity Western religion is notorious for, is a sick and debilitating way of convicting the world of sin. It is anti-productive of new life, paralyzing rather than freeing the person. Jesus does not convict the world of sin by emphasizing its guilt but by being grace to it.

Jesus' style of convicting the world of sin is reflected in St. John's notion of judgment. For John, "the believer is not judged but the unbeliever is already judged by his unbelief."[4] The judgment of Jesus is not a police-like searching out and punishing of evil acts. Jesus does not call people into their sins but out of them. The very presence of Jesus is grace—the empowerment and call to live in a new way. When we respond to this call, Jesus is grace to us. When we do not, he is judgment. He convicts us of sin by steadfastly presenting us the possibility to convert. In this way, humankind judges itself. God's judgment which is revealed in Jesus is love, a love which abides forever. Humankind's judgment on itself may be quite different. Whatever each individual decision might be, the paradox is that Jesus convicts the world of sin by the fact that he is grace.

That judgment is the reverse side of grace is grounded in the Old Testament symbol of the Wrath of God. The Wrath of God is not flagrant anthropomorphism, not a literal divine emotion alongside and opposing his love. It is a powerful symbol which recognizes that humankind can continue to resist the invitation of forgiving love. When the love of God is spurned, it appears wrathful because it is not the origin of new life but the abiding reminder that dead life still rules. The experience of God has always been a two-edged sword. At the center of exhilarating joy is the conviction that we are not who we should be. Isaiah's words upon encountering Yahweh are, "I am a man of unclean lips and live among a people of unclean lips."[5] The recognition of God's activity in Jesus leads Peter to say, "Depart from me for I am a sinful man."[6] Much can be learned about the style of God from the fact that Jesus does not leave Peter. This "staying with" of God brings out the full horror of sin. When we do not respond, grace not only becomes judgment but continual conviction which the always-present God proclaims. The fabled pursuit of humankind by God is perhaps too splendidly imaged in Francis Thompson's noble *Hound of Heaven*. Divine activity in human life is more like a bulldog, hanging in there till the end.

The presence of grace reveals and challenges the structures of sin in the self and in society. In the summer of 1974, the faculty and students of The Pastoral Institute for Social Ministry at Notre Dame experienced a graced presence that convicted the world of sin. Mother Teresa, a woman who has

dedicated herself to Jesus Christ in the poor and
starving of India, came to talk. In images and
stories, without pretention or rhetoric, she talked of
her work, of doing "something beautiful for God."
She did not berate wealthy lifestyles or the fat-cat
church or the all too affluent priests and sisters. She
merely told her story. Yet her very presence challenged self-centeredness and smug worlds and
blithe dismissals of human pain. Response to her
was not adolescent enthusiasm to go to India and
help the poor. In fact the program was considered
too individual, neglecting the systemic causes of
hunger and poverty. Yet it was so obvious that her
life and work was guided by a love which Christians claim moves the sun and stars, that all the
non-love became glaringly evident. Like Jesus, the
people who effectively convict the world of sin are
not the crusaders who scream about other people's
evil but those whose lives proclaim an alternative.

The follower of Jesus lives in the grace-judgment
paradox. The more deeply he enters into the experience of the sacred the more he is aware of his own
personal evil and the destructive forces in society.
The fact that he is alive to what is possible for
humankind sharpens his sense that we are fallen
people. The awareness of sin is the inevitable
consequence of having met grace. With this understanding, sin is not too negative as so many modern
Catholics seem to imply. To focus on sin is not to
exclude God's love but to concentrate on it as it
encounters the fickleness and generosity of the
human heart. This grace-judgment dynamic reveals
that the center of Christian life is repentance. This

does not mean that the distinguishing mark of the Christian is breast-beating. Feeling sorry, acknowledging guilt, and prolonging regret may be components of the human condition but they are not what Jesus means by repentance. Repentance is the response to grace that overcomes the past and opens onto a new future. Repentance distinguishes Christian life as one of struggle and conversion and pervades it, not with remorse, but with hope. The message of Jesus is not "Repent" but "Repent for the Kingdom of God is near."

This interlocking dynamic of grace and judgment is indispensable background to understanding the style of Jesus' challenge to repent. What makes Jesus grace and therefore judgment is that he is a Jew of the First Commandment. For Jesus, the Covenant God is the Lord his God and there are no other gods before him. As the prophets might say, this command is not only on his lips but written in his heart. Every breath Jesus draws tells the story of God. His overriding concern and the organizing center of his personality and activity is He who sent him. All praise is directed Godward. ("Why do you call me good? Only God is good.")[7] All healing power comes from the hands of God. ("If I cast out devils by the finger of God, then know that the Kingdom of God has come among you.")[8] Jesus' concern is with the will of the Father which is his food and drink, with the activity of the Father which transforms human life, and with the name of the Father which is to be hallowed. In proclaiming the good news the early church will switch focus and center directly on Jesus. In Bultmann's phrase,

"The Proclaimer becomes the One Proclaimed."
But the realization is never lost that Jesus' concentration is not on himself but what God is doing
in and through him. The liturgy preserves this
mediatory relationship of Jesus to the Father when
it urges us to pray *through* Christ our Lord.

The disciples' awareness of Jesus' unswerving
commitment to God gives birth to the premier
symbol of his identity—Son of God. After four hundred years of Christological controversy, Son of
God, with full-blown mythological and ontological
extensions, becomes the orthodox expression of
who Jesus is. Yet it is very unlikely that Jesus ever
directly called himself the Son of God. But the
evangelists, writing from a faith perspective,
placed the title on the lips of almost everyone else.
At his baptism the Heavenly Voice proclaims him
the Beloved Son. Satan plays upon his possible
sonship, "If you are the Son of God, command that
these stones be made bread."[9] The suffering de-
moniac asks him, "What do you want of me, Jesus
Son of the Most High?"[10] Peter acknowledges,
"You are the Son of the living God."[11] The high
priest interrogates, "So you are the Son of God
then?"[12] The centurion proclaims "This man indeed was the Son of God."[13] The Gospels bring
together a bizarre chorus—a Heavenly Voice,
Satan, a madman, Peter, a priest, and a centurion
—to claim sonship for Jesus. This is the evangelist's
way of affirming the intimacy of Jesus with the
Father, his radical appropriation of the first command of God to the people of Israel.

It is often suggested that Jesus does not directly

claim sonship because for him sonship is not a dignity to be claimed but a responsibility to be fulfilled. This understanding of sonship springs from the heart of the Hebrew tradition. Only in the first instance did the Father-Son relationship denote a biological fact, something given once and for all. Its fullest expression was a living relationship of paternal love evoking filial love, paternal authority evoking filial obedience. The obedient son was transparent to the father. The more obedient the son was the more the father could be seen in him. Proof of sonship was not in geneology but in listening obedience. Two incidents in the New Testament bring out this functional understanding of sonship.

In the temptation sequences, Satan wants Jesus to fall back on his prerogatives. The subtlety of the temptation is to seduce Jesus to presume on a static, irrevocable sonship and then tempt God to affirm it miraculously. Satan is asking Jesus to abandon a sonship which is a project carried out by free human decisions and rest in a sonship which is a brute fact to be exploited. Satan is hoping for a reenactment of the desert experience of Israel, the prime example of faithless and spoiled sonship. The Jews of the desert trek forced Moses to tempt God, to ask for a sign and so prove once and for all, "Is the Lord among us or not?"[14] Two of Jesus' temptations involve this same type of God-baiting. They begin with the question, "If you are the Son of God" and end with asking for a phenomenal feat. They hope to uncover an untrusting heart in Jesus. But Jesus' answer is that proof of sonship is not in exercising supernatural muscle but in not tempting the Father. He is the Son who trusts and listens and so allows God to be his Father.

The Johannine Jesus clearly states the relationship of Father to Son: "If I am not doing my Father's work, there is no need to believe me; but if I am doing it, then even if you refuse to believe in me, at least believe in the work I do; then you will know for sure that the Father is in me and I am in the Father."[15] To be a Son is to image forth the mind, heart, and soul of the Father. In this way, the Son represents the Father in the world of human transactions. He does not usurp the role of the Father or seek to permanently replace him. Rather he speaks for the Father and is called upon to act in the Father's stead. The mild rebuke which Jesus gives to Philip reveals the early Church's growing understanding of the unique relationship of Jesus to God. "Philip, how long have you been with me and you do not know that he who sees me sees the Father?"[16]

This Hebraic understanding of sonship is in close accord with contemporary sensibilities. It emphasizes that Jesus' unique relationship with God, his First Commandment character, is worked out in space and time and is the result of human decision as well as divine initiative. This understanding of Jesus in dynamic, historical terms is in marked contrast to the static categories of Greek metaphysics. Within that traditional philosophical system natures, which are unchangeable, are prior to and determinative of all action. Being precedes and governs the possibility of action. The current thrust in historical and process thought is that humankind has its being in action. No abstract, unhistorical, atemporal nature is posited. Humankind comes to be in the temporal interplay of individual decision and historical determination. From the perspective of the religious dimension, personal and social events are constituted in the interaction of God's ideal aim and humankind's subjective response. As is its wont, Christian faith has employed this thinking in understanding the relationship of Jesus to God, that is, in understanding how Jesus is grace. An investigation of Jesus through historical and process insights will help delineate the precise nature of his challenge to repent.

The historicist perspective seeks to ground the relationship of Jesus to God in time and history and not in eternity.[17] The fundamental emphasis is that humankind comes to be in relation to others. Descartes' theory that the self is first constituted in thought and only secondarily moves toward the world grossly underestimates the dynamic of human development. Personal life, first and always, is relational. The person comes to be in reciprocal and dynamic interchange. The reliance on the presence of others, indeed on their gracious initiative, is absolutely necessary for personal selfhood. Each person's selfhood results from internalizing others in a human way. This process of taking on another's characteristics, values, and behavior is especially evident in childhood. The child becomes himself by imitating the language and mannerisms of the parents. This process has many concrete manifestations. A young boy may have many toys to play with but nothing is more fascinating than his father's golf clubs. A young girl may have many dolls but nothing is more important that to dress up in her mother's clothes. The process of internalization continues into adulthood but becomes more complex and selective. The others that are internalized are carefully chosen, "significant others." Also the situation becomes dialogic. The developing person becomes a personal internalized influence in the becoming of another. In this complex process of coming to be, it should not be forgotten that selfhood, before it becomes a fascinating project, is fundamentally a gift.

The selfhood of Jesus is constituted by his relationship to God. The Father has graciously initiated the relationship and Jesus has responded and internalized the will of the Father into his own selfhood. This does not indicate a supernatural happening and the claim that Jesus is an ontological oddity should not be rushed into. It simply affirms that making God your personal center is one of the myriad ways to develop a human identity. The key word is development, for the centering of personal life in God is not a one decision affair. It is a life-long process of cumulative choices and actions. The overall impression of the Gospels is that Jesus "*grew in age, wisdom and grace before God and man.*"[18] The story of Jesus' teaching in the temple was meant to show his early awareness of God's role in human life but it is certainly not Little Lord Jesus replete with the beatific vision. The full humanity of Jesus implies that he was not abstracted from the normal temporal and developmental processes. Positively, it should be stressed in Wellhausen's famous reminder—"Jesus is a Jew." He is part of a historical people and the Father whom he learns about and whom he internalizes is the God of Abraham, Isaac and Jacob. Jesus realizes not what has never been known, and hears not what has never been spoken, but the God of the Hebrew tradition who comes to him through the Scriptures, worship, and prayer life of his people. It is through human development and human society that God initiates his loving relation to Jesus.

From a Whiteheadian perspective, John Cobb goes more deeply into the constitution of the "I" of Jesus.[19] Cobb is interested in understanding Jesus' selfhood in such a way that his claims to authority are justified. In the Gospels Jesus often hints at this authority. When criticized for carousing with tax collectors and sinners, he told the parable of the generous householder (God) who paid the last the same as the first. This ploy of defending his own actions by relating a story of how God acts, involves a tremendous personal claim. At other times the claim was more direct as when he took on the Yahwistic function of forgiving sins. The unique authority Jesus claimed is summarized in his use of the word "Amen."

> Whereas the Jew concluded his prayer to God with Amen, thus expressing his faith that God would act, Jesus prefaces his words with an 'Amen', thus denoting that prior to his utterance there is his total engagement to the act of God, of which his words thus become the channel.[20]

In short, Jesus spoke with an authority which was at the same time the authority of God.

This sense of authority differs markedly from that of the prophets. They responded to the divine "I" but always saw it over and against them as a demand to be met. Between their own will and the divine will there was always an excruciating tension. Jesus, at least at certain key moments, did not merely respond to God's will but identified with it. The basis of this identity and consequent authority was the constitution of Jesus' selfhood. The "I" of Jesus, which is the organizing center for his experiences, was constituted by the prehension of God in terms of that which makes him God—his love and lordship. Prehension is a Whiteheadian term which means the grasping and taking into account of other entities.

> This prehension was not experienced by Jesus as information about God but as the presence of God to and in him. Furthermore, and most uniquely, it was not experienced by him as one prehension alongside others to be integrated by him into a synthesis with them. Rather this prehension of God constituted in Jesus the center from which everything else in his psychic life was integrated.[21]

John Cobb suggests that this is the type of relationship which constituted the selfhood of Jesus.

A second historicist emphasis is that humankind comes to be in the carrying-out of projects. People not only create their selfhoods in interpersonal and societal relationship but within volitional strivings. The various powers, talents, and faculties of each person are marshalled and disciplined to pursue a goal. For example, a young man wants to be a radio announcer. He attends Columbia Broadcasting School, takes voice and speech lessons, learns to write intelligible copy, etc. All other possible activities—leisure time, a part time job, an avocational interest in tinkering with cars—are restricted and subordinated to the overall project of broadcasting. This concrete vocational decision is the result of the interplay of various influences —parental expectations, a personal estimate of abilities, other job possibilities, how meaningful the work is, the pay it offers. But a successful vocational choice does not solely depend on sincerity and energy. The person confronts a whole range of prior objective factors. His choice presupposes that broadcasting jobs are available, his personal gifts match the job demands, the industry will not collapse, and the basic institutions of society will remain stable. The carrying-out of a project involves an interchange between what the existing situation offers and what the person chooses.

The carrying-out of a project can be used to focus the relationship of Jesus to God. The Gospels suggest a volitional unity between Jesus and God. Jesus is a man of single purpose, willing what God wills. This does not mean his vocational struggles were unreal. Not "to set his face towards Jerusalem" was a real option. His stern rebuke to Peter when he suggests an alternative route, "Get behind me, Satan,"[22] is the anger of a man who knows how easily things get betrayed. His surrender in Gethsemane, "Not my will but your will be done,"[23] involves all the anguish of human decision. Nevertheless, Jesus is steadfast in the will of the Father. But this steadfastness must be seen as being grounded in a previous faithfulness of God. It is

God's history of prodigal love for Israel which solicits and holds the will of Jesus. It is not only Jesus'
teethgrinding endurance, but a larger set of circumstances, namely, God's predilection, which binds
them together in a common project. Just as Jesus'
selfhood is a gift from the other Jesus, his steadfastness is primarily a response to God's election
and fidelity.

A third characteristic of the historical person is
openness to the future. There is a sense in which the
past and present decisions determine the future.
And today's rational person, with high control
needs, goes to frantic extremes to manage the future, to make sure tomorrow holds as little surprise
as possible. But there is a "point beyond which," an
unforeseen that lurks in the best laid plans of mice
and men. The future flies into us, impinges on us
from beyond, demands we reckon with the pre-
cariousness of our existence. If we are dependent on
the other for our selfhood and the larger set of conditions for our strivings to be successful, we are
equally dependent on the future for the gift of life.
Will we live or die? What awaits us? This historical
condition of humankind can cripple us with anxiety
or cause us to withdraw into comfortable fantasies.
Jesus faces the future with the total trust that the
purposes of God will be fulfilled. God will bring
about his Kingdom and if this means Jesus must
die, so be it. Jesus gives himself without reserve to
whatever God will ask of him. The ground of Jesus'
trust in the future is the sovereignty of God's present activity in him and in the world. The stress is
equally on God's reassuring and confident activity

and Jesus' resulting commitment. The unique relationship of Jesus to God is that the future of Jesus is totally handed over to the future of God. John Dunne underlines both the radical and very human dimension of this trust.

> I tend to see Jesus primarily in terms of his human development and I would see him as not conceiving himself as God but as man. A man who is finding God's call for him and in discovering what God wants of him, he finds further and deeper dimensions and in the end finds that he is God: he proves to be God. . . . And so at the end, on the cross, when he uses those words of the psalm—you know, "My God, my God why have you forsaken me"—I think what he experiences there is everything crashing in on what he's tried to do—only a few have turned to this God of his and he sees this whole thing as failing and God's designs are dark at this point. So he doesn't perceive what is God's design in this. But he continues to trust in God in the face of darkness. [24]

A second contemporary attempt to express the "no other gods before him" character of Jesus employs process philosophy. A great deal of emphasis is placed on the idea that Jesus' uniqueness is one of inclusion not exclusion. Exclusion means that Jesus is unique by way of exception and poses no parallels and similarities with other events. Inclusion means that the values and qualities which appear elsewhere are found in an eminent manner in Jesus. A more precise way of stating this is that formerly God relates to Jesus in the same way that he relates to all of humankind but materially (the content of the relationship) the relationship is unique. In process thought, God relates to humankind by supplying an ideal aim for them and the situation in which they find themselves. Every event is initially constituted by this ideal aim which humankind to a greater or lesser extent actualizes. Every event comes to be in the interplay of God's ideal aim and humankind's subjective response.

The Christian claim is that Jesus is God's decisive action within history. This uniqueness must be grounded from the side of God in supplying an ideal aim and from the side of Jesus in responding to the full. God's ideal aim is relative to any particular situation. This point can be grasped by employing Hartshorne's analogy: God is to the world as the self is to the body. In this way every event is an act of God, just as every bodily action is to some extent an act of the self. But some bodily actions are particularly conducive to expressing the inner nature of the self and others are not. David Griffin uses the example of a helping man.[25] Some situations reveal this man's inner being as helpful, eg. he stops on the road to assist a fellow traveler. Other situations, eg. tying his shoes, by their very nature cannot express his inner being as a helping man. So an event can only be a special act of God if God's initial aim is that it be so. The initial aim of the event of the life, death, and resurrection of Jesus is that it be uniquely expressive of the being of God. So Jesus, because of God's singular aim for him, is unique in kind. Also Jesus fully responded to and actualized God's aim. Therefore, because of his perfect use of freedom, he is unique in degree. Process thought safeguards Christian faith in the initiative of God in terms of ideal aim and in the humanity of Jesus in terms of his free response.

These insights, taken from historicist and process approaches to human experience, unpack for us the way in which Jesus is a Jew of the First Commandment. He has his identity in relation to the Father: his project is God's project: God's future is his willing tomorrow. His freedom pursues wholeheartedly God's ideal aim. In this way the very presence of Jesus is grace because he is so "tight" with the Father that to encounter Jesus is to meet God. Therefore, in the context of the grace-judgment dynamic, Jesus convicts us of not being listening sons and daughters, of pushing the Father to the periphery of our selfhood, of pursuing our own devisive projects, of establishing a fearful future, and of not shaping our situation to its best possibility. In short, the charge is idolatry. The Jew of the First Commandment, grounded in God, inevitably calls attention to clay feet. The Jesus of singular loyalty who has no other god before Yahweh uncovers our multi-allegiances and the idols which, Calvin suggests, the mind incessantly manufactures. The Jesus who threw himself into the world and relentlessly pursued the redemption of his situation reveals that we stand and wait. Jesus' challenge to repent is a call to the lifelong death-resurrection task of overcoming the false security of our idols and truly centering ourselves in God. This will bring the freedom and the courage to realize the finest possibility of the human situation.

Idolatry has come a long way since the golden calf. Today, idolatry signifies nothing so simple and direct as dalliance with the priestess of Astarte or fashioning a pillar in honor of Baal. Fundamentally, idolatry is a false centering of the self, an ultimate investment in that which is not ultimate. Paul Tillich has stated it most precisely, "Idolatry is the elevation of a preliminary concern to ultimacy. Something essentially conditioned is taken as unconditional, something essentially partial is boosted into universality, and something essentially finite is given infinite significance (the best example is the contemporary idolatry of religious nationalism)."[26] Closely related to religious nationalism as an idolatrous social construct is utopianism. Utopianism too quickly identifies a limited, humanly-imagined future with God's future. Many political and social visions claim they are sponsored by the Gospel Jesus. This is, of course, a suspect endorsement from a Jew who himself allowed the mysterious, always-surprising will of God to be his only future.

But idolatry does not necessarily have to be the strident and militaristic brand. In fact in the lives of most people idolatry is not a raucous divinization of a cause but quiet and complete dedication to unquestioned values and systems. Theodore Roszak might not be too far off the mark in his critique of the values of technological America. Too many people give not limited but idolatrous allegiance to the building of an artificial environment.

> The life's energy of generations can be expended *developing* the thing, covering it over with concrete and plastic and sprawling supercities, finding faster ways to travel over and across its surface, consuming its substance and inventing substitutes for its depleted elements. In this busy way the time

may be passed, and we shall get used to the idolatrous life."[27]

Erich Fromm sounds a similar warning. "Our age has found a substitute for God: the impersonal calculation. This new god has turned into an idol to whom all men may be sacrificed. A new concept of the sacred and unquestionable is arising: that of calculability, probability, factuality."[28] The presence of the Jew of the First Commandment forces the question: Who gets the incense? What are you ultimately committed to and, in turn, what ultimately establishes your values and guides your actions?

Idolatry on the personal level is often manifested as "clutching." Money, sex, fame, family, another person is clutched too tightly and asked, in many cases forced, to be God. These finite things are sought not to be used and enjoyed but to secure our precarious existence. To make a thing what it is not is not to allow it to be what it is. When money is asked to secure the future, it is no longer a possession but the unquestioned ruler of the house. When sex is asked to deny time and aging, it is no longer interpersonal enjoyment but desperate moments of non-death. When another person is asked to plug all the holes in one's life, to kiss all the negativities away, companionship is impossible. The role of God which we ourselves often usurp or, what is more common but less noticed, foist on others, carries with it, in the finest primitive sense, a curse. In the garden, Satan seduces Adam and Eve with the promise, "You shall be as gods." The result of their disobedience is that they become less than human. Idolatry makes everything what it is not, distorting the relationship between self, neighbor, and God.

One tradition of the Old Testament stresses that idols, although they are nothing but wood and gold and silver, exercise demonic power over those who worship them. The psychological dynamic of idolatry is that part of the self is alienated and then deified. This part becomes an idol which jealously demands time and attention and severely constricts the life of its creator. The idol first obsesses its worshiper, then enslaves, and finally, over the years, destroys. Psalm 115 pictures the vengeance which idolatry wreaks:

> Ours is the God whose will is sovereign
> in the heavens and on earth,
> whereas their idols, in silver and gold,
> products of human skill,
> have mouths, but never speak,
> eyes, but never see,
> ears, but never hear,
> noses, but never smell,
> hands, but never touch,
> feet, but never walk,
> and not a sound from their throats.
> Their makers will end up like them,
> and so will anyone who relies on them.[29]

Idolatry cannot be isolated from human behavior, quarantined to the temple precincts, seen as only a religious aberration. The way in which our idolatrous ultimate concerns dictate our response to situations is chronicled in Langdon Gilkey's *Shantung Compound, The Story of Men and Women Under Pressure*. Gilkey was teaching in China at the outbreak of World War II. From 1943 to 1945 he was grouped with other aliens and held at a civilian internment camp near Weihsien. During those two years he kept a diary which he turned into a book in 1966. Before entering Weihsien, Gilkey formulated a question that still troubles American religion: "What real function in actual life does it [religion] perform under conditions where basic problems are dealt with by techniques and organizational skills. . . . Is there any secular use for religion, does it have any value for the common life of mankind?"[30] In November 1945, when he was released, Gilkey had the beginnings of an answer.

Two situations of pressure had occurred at Shantung Compound which revealed to Gilkey "an essential intractability on the part of the interns." Gilkey was on the quarters committee. There was a shortage of housing and his job was to parcel out an equal amount of space to everyone. He attempted to be just and fair only to find out that was the last thing that was wanted. Rational and just concerns were no match for self-interest. Everyone stole, then jealously guarded, what space they could. Intelligence was only used to rationalize and guard total self-interest. Finally, in desperation, the quarters committee had to appeal to the authority of the Japanese guards to implement fair housing.

A second situation concerned the shortage of food. Food had always been scarce but in the last months of 1944 rations were extremely low. One day 1550 packages arrived from the American Red Cross. At this time there were 1450 persons in camp, 200 of whom were Americans. The Japanese determined that everyone in the camp would receive one parcel and the Americans would receive one and one-half parcels. But a small committee of Americans claimed that the Japanese had no right distributing American Red Cross goods. They demanded all the parcels be handed over to the American community. The Japanese officials did not know what to do so they forwarded the problem to Tokyo for arbitration. In the delay, Gilkey and some of his friends surveyed the Americans to determine their real position. Some were direct, "It's American property, I'm American. I don't want to give it to any foreigners." Others talked about the legal point: "Could the Japanese really distribute American goods to foreigners?" Others roped in moral motives: "If the Japanese distribute the goods, it would be a neutral act of authority. But if the Americans were to receive all the packages and then give some to others it would be an act of virtue." What Gilkey and his friends found was overwhelming self-interest masked by reason. As with space so with food.

Gilkey theologically interprets his experience at Weihsien in terms of idolatry. Every person possesses an ultimate concern, "that center of devotion in a man's existence which provides for his life its final security and meaning, and to which, therefore, he gives his ultimate love and commitment."[31] When this ultimate concern is threatened, people act in threatened ways. If a person's ultimate concern is his own welfare or that of his group, he is no longer free to act morally under pressure. He will be driven to reinforce and defend his ultimate at all cost.

Where one ultimately lives is a good indicator of how one will act. The aphorism of Matthew Arnold that "religion is morality tinged with emotion" needs to be reversed. Gilkey claims, "A man's morality is his religion enacted in social existence."[32] Moral action or lack of it springs from the deepest center of one's being. The primordial sin is idolatry, ultimate allegiance to what is finite. From this follows the moral evils of injustice, prejudice, aggression, and dishonesty. In this context, Gilkey sees the person of faith as one "whose center of security and meaning lies not in his own life but in the power and love of God, a man who has surrendered an overriding concern for himself, so that the only really significant things in his life are the will of God and his neighbor's welfare. Such faith is intimately related to love, for faith is an inward self surrender, a loss of self centeredness and concern which transforms a man and frees him to love.[33]

Jesus, because his center is the Father, convicts us of centering ourselves elsewhere. It may be money, sex, or country we adore but more than likely idolatry begins at home. It is the self—enclosed and frightened—who gets the incense. The challenge of Jesus to repent is not initially to do good deeds or to pray more but to recenter our lives in the love of God. This movement outward understands that a person does not hold onto life with a tightly clenched fist but with an open hand. Only when it is given away, Jesus said, is life gained. To recenter in God is basically to return to creaturehood. It involves the decision to give up the pretense of omnipotence and trust the limits of human existence, no matter how fearful their appearance. Rooted in the Father, we are then free to act in a new and creative way. We do not have to scurry about clutching tenaciously to the present for fear of the future, shoring up our egos with lies and delusions.

The things we most deeply and legitimately hope for but which we can never achieve are the gifts of God. If Prometheus knew the Father of Jesus, he would not have had to steal the fire; it would have been given him. The Christian question is not how to get the fire but accepting God's gift of fire, how do we responsibly use it? God-centeredness means release from the idols which enslave us to destructive concerns and empowerment to create communities recognizable by their love. If asked how free is this person who "lives in God", the answer of Jesus is: Free enough to genuinely be for others, to walk the extra mile, to turn the other cheek, to share the last shirt, to resist not evil. This is not rampant romanticism but mind boggling images to convey the untold possibilities of the God-centered life.

A common misunderstanding is that centering life in God means giving things up. This comes from a see-saw understanding of God and the world. If God goes up, the world goes down. If the world goes up, God goes down. This faulty thinking is reinforced by the mystic principle—"If you turn away from the things of earth God will give you everything that is in Heaven." The challenge to repent is not to desert the earth but to possess it in the only way which can bring happiness—as a creature. Centered in the Father of Jesus we forsake all things as gods to be worshipped to gain them as creatures to be enjoyed. In this way we are free from the idolatrous anxiety to secure a basically insecure life by investing what is finite with the absolute powers of divinity. In themselves, the first place at table, the salutation in the marketplace, and a second and larger set of barns are merely a place to sit, a wave, and a storehouse. It is when we are ultimately committed to them, spend our lives in frenzied pursuit of them, totally define ourselves in relation to them, that we are in the unenviable predicament of the camel trying to pass through the eye of a needle. The challenge to repent is the call to make all things new, not by abandoning them, but by reappropriating them from our personal center in the Father of Jesus.

A contemporary pragmatic judgment of Jesus' challenge to repent might be that it lacked a definite program. What is needed is more of the reformer's pitch—a social platform, concrete proposals, readily achievable goals. But Jesus, with deeply religious instincts, swung his ax at the roots. He intuits the strong bond between ultimate concerns and proximate life styles. He does not confront violent behavior and oppressive structures on their own terms. He tracks them to their source of energy and inspiration in the idolatrous leanings of humankind. Jesus' hope is not solely for a different future, realignment of the ins and outs and the firsts and lasts, but for a new future. His vision is not restricted, as so many revolutionary manifestos are, to mere reversal—this time around Abel murders Cain. Jesus' excitement is that humankind does not have to return to the scene of the crime again and again with only a slightly changed scenario. Repentance means turnabout, metanoia, the radical restructuring of allegiances and priorities. If humankind recenters itself in the Father of Jesus, it can muster the freedom and courage to create a new society. The challenge of Jesus to repent is no less than this.

Chapter 4

The Challenge To Celebrate

Perhaps the most neglected line of the Gospels is the injunction of the Matthean Jesus, "Do not look dismal."[1] The Christian religionist has managed a popular reputation, not entirely unearned, for being glum. He is often serious to the point of morbidity and comes across as a tightkneed naysayer. Almost everything is "no laughing matter." Jesus' challenge to repent has been transformed with a certain amount of dark pleasure to a call to wallow in guilt. Sin lurks on the underside of every joy and we can never be too careful. Often there is a vigilante aspect to this type of personality. The person fiercely patrols human activity for wrongdoing and even moves within the mind to chastise thoughts. This caricature is reinforced by a story Groucho Marx tells. Groucho is standing on a street corner in Montreal. A priest who is passing by recognizes him and says, "Mr. Marx I want to thank you for bringing so much joy into the world. The eyebrows arch and Groucho strikes, "And I want to thank you, Father, for taking so much joy out of it."

Only the youngest Catholics do not remember the overdose of sin which drugged Catholic upbringing. Catholic spirituality was mainlining

Good Friday. Christmas sermons had a way of ending with, "Remember—the wood of the crib is the
wood of the cross." Popular forms of meditation
ingeniously combined sin and suffering. Examina-
tion of conscience was a conducted tour of the
crucified Christ. His thorn-pierced head reminded
us of our sinful thoughts; his wounded side revealed the lecherous desires of our hearts; his nail-
pierced hands and feet asked where our hands had
been and where our feet had taken us. The transla-
tion into English of Durwell's book *The Resurrection*
in 1960 had a tremendous impact in American circles. It jolted people into an awareness of how con-
stricted Catholic spirituality had become. That
Christ was risen was not only good but to American
Catholics it was news.

Not balancing the cross with the resurrection,
damning sin but not celebrating grace, leads to
aberrations in both the personal and social orders.
A person whose controlling self-image is "sinner"
is prone to lead a fearful life. If everything is seen
from its imperfect side, from the inevitable fact that
even the best efforts fall short, nothing much is
ventured. Emotions are distrusted; motivations are
suspect; human contact is contaminated. What develops is a hunched, frightened stance towards life.
Nicolas Berdyaev's comment is borne out: "One
who lives in constant terror at his own sins is powerless to accomplish anything in the world."[2] An
interesting example of sin consciousness and social
policy is Robert Heilbroner's recent book *An In-
quiry Into the Human Prospect*. Heilbroner, a long-
time liberal, carefully details humankind's wrong-

headedness. We are contemporary Samsons pulling the world down around us and what we need to be are Atlases, bearing its weight. The only solution, Heilbroner's reluctant conclusion, is fascism. To stare long and exclusively at humankind's sinfulness brings the social temptation to curb freedom and institute dictatorship.

If the cross without the resurrection breeds deep pessimism, the resurrection without the cross generates unfounded optimism. For many Catholics an exclusive sin consciousness is yesterday's hangup, nostalgia at best; but an exclusive resurrection consciousness is today's temptation. This is the flower and balloon mentality that glibly passes over the heartlessness and intractability of the world. The theological rallying cry is, "Christ is risen!" Paul sternly confronts this attitude in the Church at Corinth. The Corinthians were living exclusively out of a theology of the resurrection. They were the first realized eschatologists. The Kingdom had fully come; the Spirit fully possessed them; they spoke in tongues, the language of the angels and the world to come. The resurrection of the dead was an afterthought, for eternal life was this ecstatic, Spirit-filled moment. As Kasemann points out, "Anyone who feels himself to be a citizen of heaven and permeated with heavenly strength no longer needs to take the earth seriously."[3] Paul complements this theology with an emphasis on the cross of Christ. For Paul, the cross is more than the last occurrence in the life of Jesus before the beginning of his glorious risen life. The risen and exalted Christ remains the crucified Jesus. He whom you experience as risen is precisely he who is crucified. Paul's theology of the resurrection, like the Corinthians', stresses freedom. But for Paul, the freedom is not angelic release from the earth. It is a cruciform freedom which suffers all the indignities of human existence and struggles to transform them. Martin Luther ridicules the enthusiastic Corinthians of his day as people "who have swallowed the Holy Spirit, feathers and all."[4] Perhaps a too blunt and unfair retort to resurrection mania is, "Christ may have risen but you have not."

Resurrection living can easily degenerate into euphoria. Personal and social evil is not looked at; or when it is, it is a rose-colored vision. There is no realization of the gut ambiguities and tragic comedies which fill all our days. No one notices the effort at love which ends in manipulation; the dialogue that subtly dominates; the major truth with a lie at the center. The enthusiast seems on an unwarranted high, puffed up with a joy that has not been payed for. The knowledge that there is no such thing as a free lunch shocks him. If sin consciousness frowns too consistently at the best efforts of the self and neighbor, resurrection consciousness smiles too often and at all the wrong times. The whole impression is of a fragile world made by people with thin hands and bloodless voices.

In the socio-political arena the enthusiast lacks stamina. He is not equipped for the long haul and he will not endure the many winters it takes to effectively change structures and attitudes. The enthusiast tends to believe the world is malleable to the tender request. Reason and love are quick and sure winners over apathy and intransigency. The counter culture of the late sixties had many of the characteristics of resurrection mania. Their naivete and resulting disillusionment is captured in a stanza from a recent poem.

> Why did not the tearless city descend to earth
> when we held hands on the boulevard of song?
> Why did not the fist open and bomb bay close
> when we played naked in the meadows and lakes?
> The hawk still swoops: the undaunted
>   serpent spits.
> Are we left with a chemical Eden, or a patch
> of monastery to make too much of,
>   or the deadening prospect
> of a raise after three months and
>   the sad memory of youth:
> I once saw Christ on a white horse.[5]

What is clear from this analysis is that the cross and resurrection, sin and celebration, must be constantly juxtaposed. If either one dominates, the struggle character of human existence is lost. What has been created is either heaven (celebration) or hell (sin) and what is lost is the earth as a field of existential decision and growth. Yet given religious people's penchant for extremes, balance is difficult to achieve. Christian history is a swing from resurrection mania to sin saturation. The pendulum seldom rests at center. In this oscillating context people would probably be more comfortable relating Jesus to sin consciousness. There is respect and reverence for a sad-countenanced character, stoop shouldered from the burden of our sins and red-eyed from weeping over Jerusalem. A haunted, brooding Jesus shaking his head and pronouncing interminable woes appeals to us. Someone stricken by life's evils and in pain over human waywardness supplies the proper seriousness and concern for God. In this drear and melancholy atmosphere the laughing Jesus challenges us to celebrate.

Jesus was not Tom Jones, as some try to make him, but neither was he John the Baptist. As Jesus pointed out, his style was markedly different from the Baptist's. "For John the Baptist came neither eating bread nor drinking wine and you say, 'He is possessed.' The Son of Man came eating and drinking and you say, 'Look at him, a glutton and a drinker, a friend of tax gatherers and sinners'."[6] When asked why his disciples did not fast like John's, Jesus left no doubt about his celebrative life style. "Can you expect mourning when the bridegroom is with them?"[7] Jesus' ministry was not distinguished by desert fasts but by table fellowship which symbolized the advent of the Kingdom of God. It must be remembered that the foremost scriptural symbol for heaven is not the beatific vision but a festive party.

Joy is a constant theme in the parables of Jesus. Jesus told the story of the treasure buried in the field in response to the question, "How should the Kingdom be received?" The Palestinian background of this parable illumines its meaning. Palestine, because of its geographical location, was a corridor between the conquering empires of the ancient world. In a land so frequently plundered, wealthy people would often bury their valuables for safe-keeping. The dream of every poor tiller of the soil was that one day his hoe would strike a solid object. He would dig up a chest and discover a fabulous treasure. Then *in his joy* he would sell all he has, buy the field, and change his whole way of life to suit his new-found wealth. Jesus' point is that the Kingdom should be experienced with the wild joy of a poor peasant who is suddenly rich and free. A contemporary image in the same vein might be Zero Mostel in *Fiddler on the Roof* strutting with happiness and singing, "If I Were a Rich Man." The unbounded joy of the poor milkman at the thought of riches is the type of exhilarating joy the Kingdom brings.

For Jesus, repentance itself is a joyous occasion and calls for celebration. In his fifteenth chapter Luke brings together three of Jesus' parables which closely relate the challenge to repent and the challenge to celebrate. In each parable something is lost and then found again—a coin, a sheep, and a son. When the housewife finds the coin, she invites her friends in to celebrate. When the shepherd recovers the sheep, he calls in his neighbor and says "Rejoice with me! For I have found my lost sheep."[8] And the prodigal father of the wastrel son puts a ring on his son's finger, sandals on his feet, fits him out in the finest robe, and kills the fatted calf. For Jesus, repentance always ends in a party which celebrates life over death. The oriental father knows the imperative of joy. He chides the reluctant older brother, "We had to celebrate and be glad because your brother was dead and has come back to life."[9] But the festivities are not confined to the repentant one and his friends. Luke ends the parable of the lost coin and lost sheep with a heavenly scene of

God and the angels rejoicing. Perhaps Chesterton is correct and God hid his mirth from us because we would have been overwhelmed. But close to mirth is joy which is the unmistakable characteristic of the welcoming Father and the parables of his Son.

Jesus sports an attitude and style which mixes joy, courage, and freedom. The Middle Ages dubbed this virtue *hilaritas*. It is a joyful confidence, an affirmation of life even in the face of diminishment. It is the celebration of the supper before betrayal and crucifixion, the insistence of the Kingdom of another world while in chains before the King of this world, the talk of paradise while nailed to the tree of rejection. *Hilaritas* is a freedom which does not allow the circumstances of life to totally dictate feelings and moods. The spirit of *hilaritas* runs through Jesus' put-down of worry:

> That is why I am telling you not to worry about your life and what you are to eat, nor about your body and how you are to clothe it. Surely life means more than food, and the body more than clothing! Look at the birds in the sky. They do not sow or reap or gather into barns; yet your heavenly Father feeds them. Are you not worth much more than they are? Can any of you, for all his worrying, add one single cubit to his span of life? And why worry about clothing? Think of the flowers growing in the fields; they never have to work or spin; yet I assure you that not even Solomon in all his regalia was robed like one of these. Now if that is how God clothes the grass in the field which is there today and thrown into the furnace tomorrow, will he not much more look after you, you men of little faith? So do not worry; do not say, "What are we to eat? What are we to drink? How are we to be clothed?" It is the pagans who set their hearts on all these

things. Your heavenly Father knows you need them all. Set your hearts on his kingdom first, and on his righteousness, and all these other things will be given you as well. So do not worry about tomorrow: tomorrow will take care of itself. Each day has enough trouble of its own.[10]

This enduringly beautiful passage does not purport an economic vision or give practical advice on long term planning. It is *hilaritas'* playful reminder not to let worry be the whole story about life. It is faith's persistent proclamation—fret ye not.

Hilaritas is not frivolity. It is not a flightiness which is smugly unconcerned with oppression and suffering. *Hilaritas* is passionately involved with the pain of the world but not absorbed by it. It takes life seriously but not ultimately. It strains for betterment but at the moment of disaster it may wink. *Hilaritas* is Zorba and his boss dancing on the shores of the Aegean after their lignite mine has collapsed and they have lost everything. The heart of *hilaritas* is a paradox.

One aspect accepts each person's mud base, ridicules divine ambitions, and meditates on the maxim, "Who by thinking it can add one cubit to his stature." It is the comic insight which notices "the man who is straining to divinize himself . . . is packing a little extra weight. Though he is on his way to infinity, he has a ham sandwich in his pocket and a bandage on one big toe."[11] This aspect of *hilaritas* which understands that humankind transcends only in inches is juxtaposed by the ambition to be faithful to the gift of God's love which it has received. *Hilaritas* is permeated with joyous confidence and so possesses the courage and freedom to surprise the world with new acts of love. A master washes the feet of his disciples; a Samaritan helps a Jew; a Jew shares both faith and meal with a Gentile. *Hilaritas* is acceptance and transcendence in the same breath.

The source of Jesus' celebrative life style is his joyous trust in the activity of God. Joachim Jeremias calls this the Great Assurance. The Great Assurance is reflected in the parables of the mustard seed and the leaven. Both these parables are responses to doubts about the coming Kingdom. How could a ragtail band of Galilean peasants be the revelation of God's activity? The disciples were dismayed that people were not responding wholeheartedly. They were passing them by to purchase farms and marry wives and sell oxen. Preaching the Kingdom was not as easy as it seemed in the first flush of enthusiasm. Success was neither quick enough nor sure enough. Jesus' response to these doubts is to live in hope and not discouragement. The mustard seed is the smallest of all seeds yet one day it is a magnificent bush. The leaven is tiny but it permeates and raises the entire mass of dough. To the modern mind, this might suggest the process of growth but Jesus' point is contrast. He stresses the miracle of difference between an insignificant beginning and a glorious end. This Great Assurance that God will see His purposes through is the source of Jesus' freedom. This does not mean that Jesus knows the future but only that he trusts it. His confidence is not the crystal ball variety but the conviction that the God who is coming to be in him is faithful to his promises. St. Paul expresses this same confidence in a classic passage: "For I am certain of this: neither death nor life, nor angel, nor prince, nothing that exists, nothing still to come, not any power, or height or depth, nor any created thing, can ever come between us and the love of God made visible in Christ Jesus our Lord."[12]

The earliest Gospel accounts leave no doubt that the disciples, although in the footsteps of the master, were quite far behind. In them, Jesus' joyous trust was distorted into political victory and personal glory. They only dimly surmised what Jesus clearly saw—the question, which one will be first, meant who has the courage to be last. Jesus' confidence in the activity of God was matched by their hesitancy. He moved forward to meet an unknown future: they lurked in the shadows waiting to see the shape of tomorrow before committing themselves today. In this context the death of Jesus shattered the community of his followers. Strike the shepherd, the prophet says, and the sheep scatter. The Great Assurance was countered by the Great Disillusionment. In the minds of the disciples the death of Jesus not only ended his physical life but murdered the truth he believed in. The cross is emblematic of Jesus' entire ministry. In one final violent stroke it poses the ultimate religious question which throughout his life Jesus had witnessed to! Can the last power of life be gracious if this man is crucified? Was the joyous confidence which characterized Jesus merely whistling in the dark? Was he wrong? Does the sparrow fall and no one cares? Are the hairs of our heads left uncounted?

What manner of love allows this—Pilate dies in his bed and Jesus is nailed to the wood? "If you are the Son of God, come down from the cross" is not only the taunt of the high priest but the deepest question of the disciples.

The resurrection, the disciples' experience of the continued yet transformed presence of Jesus, answers these questions. The resurrection looks backward to the pre-Easter Jesus and proclaims him and his message true. The Great Assurance which was voided by the Great Disillusionment is restored by the Great Vindication. The early Church's initial interpretation of the resurrection may be paraphrased—what men have rejected God has accepted. Jesus has proved the clue to the meaning of human existence, the pathway to the Really Real, the revelation of eternal life. The demonic powers of the world and our own terrifying evil will not win the day. Our brother Jesus has broken their hold, not with dragon-slaying strength, but by living the love of God amid the ambiguities of existence. An ancient custom of the Greek Orthodox Church reserves the day after Easter for laughter and hilarity. On this day the sanctuary is filled with festivity and joking to celebrate the cosmic joke God pulled on Satan in the resurrection. The resurrection is the source of Christian joy and celebration, the music to which we ceaselessly dance, the song which we forever sing.

A faulty understanding of the resurrection suggests it is a solution to human existence. The experience of the continued yet transformed presence of Jesus makes things perfectly clear, endows the

Christian with supernatural knowledge about the world to come. The Christian no longer thrashes about in a drowning existence but calmly sails for home. With this understanding the distinguishing mark of the Christian is that he is well-informed. But the resurrection does not explain away the mystery of God and humankind but proclaims it to be real and quickens people's entry into it. The resurrection may be the primordial Christian religious experience, the Father of faith, and the confounder of evil but it is not the dispeller of mystery. It would be true to say the resurrection left the disciples as stunned as the crucifixion. The monumental difference is the crucifixion stunned them into sorrow and lethargy and the resurrection into joy and mission. The resurrection, like all of Jesus' actions is an invitation to overcome death by plunging life irretrievably into the mystery of God and humankind. In this way the resurrection, while not a solution in any grossly simplistic sense, directs our consciousness to the overcoming of fate and death, to the sudden intrusions of beauty in our life, and to celebrating the future in such a way that it shapes the present.

Easter is an invitation into a universe of possibilities. It is not that the old universe of entrapment has disappeared. In fact, it is all too much with us but its death grip on our throat has been loosened. The blind and most often cruel decrees of fate are no longer Lord in this world. The terrors of history, the most calamitous turn of events, a sudden and meaningless crucifixion do not have the final word. The ultimate mystery which informs and guides our personal mysteries is resurrecting love. Each person's story is not an idiot's tale. The sound has shaped itself into the Word of life and the fury, still untamed, has gathered itself into the shalom of the risen Christ. If we dwell in this resurrecting love and act out of it, no situation can destroy us. The famous concentration camp experiences of Victor Frankl come to a similar conclusion. Even in limited and oppressive situations where external freedoms are denied, a person retains the freedom to determine the attitude toward what is unavoidable. Fate and death are givens of human existence; attitudes towards them is the human task. The resurrection faith of the Christian is the basis for an attitude towards fate and death which emasculates them. It might be too much to say with Luther that they become the "veils of God";[13] yet they are no longer the brute, unyielding facts about us but realities pliant to the power of love.

When fate and death are relativized by the experience of resurrecting love, the real evil becomes clear. That which destroys humankind is that which estranges it from the ultimate love of the resurrection. Sin as the force of alienation would hand us back to the caprice of fate and the entrapment of death. It reestablishes them as God and leaves Jesus on the cross not as a symbol of suffering love but as the jeering despair that every person has about nails and lances. Sin then comes into its own not as a forbidden yet pleasurable act but as the robber of joy. The Gospel Jesus does not do away with fear as it is sometimes too glibly asserted, he focuses it. "Fear not them which kill the body but fear him who is able to destroy both the body and soul in hell."[14] What must be maintained as the source of overcoming fate and death is the relationship to God. As usual Paul says this best:

> For whether we live, we live unto the Lord
> And whether we die, we die unto the Lord.
> Whether we live, therefore, or die, we are the Lord's.[15]

The Christian celebrates that he is the Lord's and whoever is the Lord's possesses the dizzying freedom to throw life away and experience its myriad returns. The joy of the resurrection seduces the miser in each of us into spendthrift love.

Christian celebration, although rooted in the phrase of the Johannine Christ "Do not be afraid I have overcome the world,"[16] does not stop there. The resurrection of Christ alerts the Christian to sudden intrusions of beauty. The Easter Christ who proclaims, "Behold I make all things new," convinces the Christian that the world is blossoming for those with flower eyes. Wild things are happening; grace is surreptitiously at work healing our wounds; surprising invitations are being offered. The dull old world is shot through with the excitement of Christ. The resurrection appearances carry this sense of beauty and surprise. Unfortunately the appearances are most often read as scientific challenges. The questions, "Did they occur? How did they occur? In what sense are they historical?" dominate our approach to these stories. Along with the empty tomb they are cited as proof to confront the skeptical. Since they no longer seem to work as proof, we might explore them as the poetic overflow

of faith. Whatever they tell us about the risen
Christ, they also tell us how the Christian experiences life after encountering Jesus.

Like her friend
she would curse the barren tree
and glory in the lilies of the field.
She lived in noons and midnites,
in those mounting moments of high dance
when blood is wisdom and flesh love.

But now
before the violated cave
on the third day of her tears
she is a black pool of grief
spent upon the earth.

They have taken her dead Jesus,
unoiled and unkissed,
to where desert flies and worms
more quickly work.

She suffers wounds that will not heal
and enters into the pain of God
where lives the gardener
who once exalted in her perfume,
knew the extravagance of her hair,
and now asks her whom she seeks.

In Peter's dreams
the cock still crowed.
He returned to Galilee
to throw nets into the sea
and watch them sink
like memories into darkness.
He did not curse the sun
that rolled down his back
or the wind that drove
the fish beyond his nets.
He only waited for the morning
when the shore mist would lift
and from his boat he would see him.
Then after naked and impetuous swim
with the sea running from his eyes
he would find a cook

with holes in his hands
and stooped over dawn coals
who would offer him the Kingdom of God
for breakfast.

On the road that escapes Jerusalem
and winds along the ridge to Emmaus
two disillusioned youths
dragged home their crucified dream.
They had smelled messiah in the air
and rose to that scarred and ancient hope
only to mourn what might have been.
And now a sudden stranger falls upon their loss
with excited words about mustard seeds
and surprises hidden at the heart of death
and that evil must be kissed upon the lips
and that every scream is redeemed for its echoes
in the ear of God and do you not understand
what died upon the cross was fear.
They protested their right to despair but he said,
"My Father's laughter fills the silence of the tomb."
Because they did not understand they offered
    him food.
And in the breaking of the bread
they knew the impostor for who he was—
the arsonist of the heart.

After the end
comes the conspiracy
of gardeners, cooks, and strangers.[17]

The Christian has the nagging tendency to see a conspiracy. Only it is not the alliance of evil but St. Paul's contention that God is working with those who love him to bring about good. Grace is working through the most unlikely people to call us from our grief (like the gardener called Magdalene), from our guilt (like the cook called Peter), and from our disillusionment (like the stranger called the youths). John Robinson suggests that these resurrection stories might have a "peculiarly compelling power for our generation. For they all tell of one who comes unknown and uninvited into the human situation, disclosing himself as the gracious neighbor before he can be recognized as Master and Lord."[18] The gracious neighbor who becomes Christ for us (the invitation to new life) may be the contemporary entry into the Christian story. In the Gospel accounts, Jesus told what may be his most famous parable in answer to the question, "Who then is my neighbor?" The person who proved neighbor, the Samaritan, comes as a shock and surprise but one which Jesus in his radical restructuring of our consciousness insists on. The Christian celebrates because Christ may come to him today; and he may look like the butcher, the baker, the candlestick maker or even, and this we only reluctantly admit, that arrogant, self-centered, and unscrupulous person—our enemy.

The resurrection is the source of Christian celebration not only because it overcomes the negativities of existence and alerts us to our Christic identity but also because it proclaims hope for the future. One of the earliest resurrection titles given to Jesus, Son of Man, captures this dimension of future hope and establishes Christian existence as the interlude between the first and second coming of the Lord. Because this title is found in the earliest strata of the Jesus tradition and has a definitely Jewish character it has received major critical attention. One of the persistent questions is whether Jesus ever used the title of himself. An untrained reader of the gospels might immediately assert that he did. Jesus often refers to himself both in his present activity and in his coming suffering as the Son of Man. For example, "The Son of Man comes eating and drinking . . ." and "The Son of Man must suffer and be rejected by the elders, the chief priests, and the scribes, be put to death and rise three days later."[19] But there is a third group of sayings concerning the Son of Man which emphasizes his future coming in glory. In these sayings Jesus seems to distinguish himself from the Son of Man. The Son of Man is not Jesus but his vindicator, "Everyone who acknowledges me before men, the Son of Man also will acknowledge before the angels of God."[20] From this analysis the dizzying questions of scholarship arise. Did Jesus view himself as a prophet of the last times whose preaching would be validated when the Son of Man (another figure entirely) came on the clouds? With the impact and direction of the resurrection experience did the early Church recognize these two distinct figures (Jesus and the Son of Man) as one and the same? Did they then put into the mouth of Jesus the Son of Man sayings so that his real identity would not be in question? At the present moment there are no universally accepted answers to these questions nor in the future are there likely to be. Without exploring the intricate arguments perhaps Bruce Vawter's moderate estimate may be taken as a guide. The Son of Man sayings "in one form or other. . .put us in real contact with an emphasis in Jesus' own preaching."[21]

Whatever Jesus' self-understanding, in a Hebrew milieu his resurrection would immediately bring to mind the Son of Man. The Son of Man is the key figure in the seventh chapter of the Book of Daniel. The cultural matrix of this chapter is apocalypticism, a world-view greatly influenced by the dualistic philosophy of Iran. The hallmark of the Jewish apocalyptic tradition is the sharp distinction between this age and the age to come. A cataclysmic event will end this world and in its place will be a new heaven and a new earth. In Daniel's vision of the End Time he is transported to the judgment seat of God:

> Thrones were set in place
> and one of great age took his seat.
> His robe was white as snow,
> the hair of his head as pure as wool.
> His throne was a blaze of flames,
> its wheels were a burning fire.
> A stream of fire poured out,
> issuing from his presence.
> A thousand thousand waited on him,
> ten thousand times ten thousand stood before him.
> A court was held
> and the books were opened.

Before the Almighty the oppressing nations of the earth, symbolized by four beasts, come for judgment. One is slain; the others are rendered powerless and paroled for an indefinite time. Then upon the clouds comes:

> one like a son of man.
> He came to the one of great age
> and was led into his presence.
> On him was conferred sovereignty,
> glory and kingship,
> and all men of all peoples, nations and
> languages became his servants.

His sovereignty is an eternal sovereignty
which shall never pass away,
nor will his empire ever be destroyed.[22]

This "one like a son of man" is a personification of Israel. He is human rather than beastly and receives a favorable judgment rather than condemnation. In intertestamental literature this figure of the Son of Man is further elaborated and matures from a personification to an actual person. He is not only the one who has been favorably judged but he becomes the judge of the living and the dead, the good and the wicked. His coming will usher in the last days.

In this apocalyptic context the interpretation of the resurrection which immediately suggests itself is that Jesus is the Son of Man. Favorable judgment has been passed on his life. He is the one who will come upon the clouds as God's agent of judgment and redemption. Apocalypticism believed that the death of the old world and the birth of the new would befall all at the same time. With the resurrection of Jesus the script has been changed. God has worked a new creation in this one man, Jesus, who is the harbinger of the end, the first born of the dead, the pioneer of a new world. Although the new creation has occurred in only one man, it is not an isolated and freakish event. This is not merely the good fortune of an individual but a cosmic happening. We cannot go about our lives as if nothing had happened or as if what happened has no meaning for us. Jesus will return to gather in the just and scatter the wicked. The initial missionary activity of the Church was the work of grace-time, the indefinite (but probably short) period between the first and second comings of Jesus.

Today most Christians are only baffled by the title Son of Man. In twentieth century American culture the title is not recognized and carries no impact. If anything, the title has been stripped of its first century denotation and transformed into an affirmation of Jesus' humanity. This is especially true when the phrase is connected with the suffering sayings. What is more human than to suffer and die? Is this not the lot of every son of man? The Son of Man is an example of a familiar historical phenomenon. When the original meaning and context of an image is lost, a new meaning is supplied. The Son of Man is not totally discarded but its significance changes. The Son of Man which for the early Church pointed to Jesus as Anticipated End and Eschatological Judge today points to Jesus in his suffering humanity.

Even within the early Church the Son of Man did not long maintain its cultural currency. The Son of Man is incurably Semitic and for Jews a powerful symbol of the meaning of Jesus. But the early Church did not stay within the territorial boundaries of Palestine or the religious and cultural confines of the Hebrew tradition. The missionary impulse of Pentecost moved the Church outward "from Jerusalem to the ends of the earth." What was encountered was the Hellenistic-Gentile culture with its own deeply rooted religious presuppositions and experiences. In this culture the Son of Man was not an established figure in the salvific plan of God. To proclaim Jesus by relating him to the Son of Man was to explain one unknown by another. A second reason why the Son of Man lost its preeminent role in defining Jesus was the delay of the Second Coming.

In its apocalyptic framework the Son of Man, at least in the minds of many Christians, guaranteed the quick return of Jesus and the end of the world. When this did not occur, the waiting Church gradually settled into time and history. Also the experience of the Spirit in their midst pushed them to dwell in the present and not to look so exclusively to the future. With the awareness that the world was going to plod on, the image of the Son of Man lost its burning immediacy and eventually gave way to more relevant titles.

Within the contemporary Church it would be impossible and probably not desirable to reactivate the Son of Man title in all its apocalyptic glory. Yet, like so many of the traditional symbols, it contains a profound insight into Christian living. The Christian lives between memory and hope. He does not just drain the moment but celebrates a future which has already happened in Jesus. The risen Christ is the anticipated end of time. He is what humankind will look like when God's will has been fully responded to. Jesus is our hope not only because he has personally triumphed but because he calls us to live under his Lordship and so bring about in ourself the transformation which has occurred in him. It is the risen Christ who sends the Holy Spirit and the only response that can slander the Spirit is despair.

Hope founded on the resurrected Jesus enters

every Eucharistic celebration. The Eucharist is an eschatological act which proclaims the End Time, when God will be all in all. In more traditional terminology, mass is an "act of heaven." It is the placement of an act of unity (communal eating as the anticipation of the heavenly banquet) in a world of division. In doing so it enacts the future (the unity of humankind under God) in such a way that it shapes and gives direction to the present. In a Christian setting to celebrate is the severest form of critique. To enact the meaning of the resurrection of Jesus, the future union with God and communion among men, is to give notice to the hegemony of evil. Evil will not endure and shape the future, for it did not endure and shape the future of Jesus. Christian hope, celebrated eucharistically, is neither whim nor illusion but the empowerment to struggle based on the continued yet transformed presence of the resurrected Christ.

The Christian celebration of struggle within hope can be contrasted with the contemporary style of struggle within despair. In Camus' *The Plague*, Doctor Rieux and Tarrou talk about evil, humankind's response, and belief in God:

> '. . . since the order of the world is shaped by death, mightn't it be better for God if we refuse to believe in him and struggle with all our might against death, without raising our eyes toward the heaven where he sits in silence?'
> Tarrou nodded.
> 'Yes. But your victories will never be lasting; that's all.'
> Rieux's face darkened.
> 'Yes, I know that. But it's no reason for giving up the struggle.'

'No reason, I agree. Only, I now can picture what this plague must mean for you.'
'Yes, a never ending defeat.'[23]

The Christian struggles alongside Dr. Rieux but does not share his magnificent nihilism. The exhilarating feeling of dedicating oneself to a doomed cause is not his. He must settle for something less than heroic defeat—the gift of victory. The Christian is not the noble anti-hero luxuriating in despair but the child of the Kingdom, the grave-merry person who blends the perils of human freedom with the pursuing grace of God. He does not deny evil but installs it in the movement of hope. In his life, as in all life, there are tears and laughter but ultimately there is laughter, the laughter of the resurrected Christ.

Chapter 5

The Challenge To Trust

If a minimal, perhaps facetious, statement could be made about the impact of Jesus on his disciples, it would be: After him things were never the same. The New Testament goes to elaborate extent to make this point, often with great literary flourish. The structure of the first, and beginning of the second, chapters of John's Gospel parallel the Genesis account of creation. In the artistic construct of seven days—from the Baptist as messianic herald through the choosing of the disciples to their confirmation in faith at Cana—the Spirit once again broods over chaos and brings forth a new creation. The man who met his Lord on the road to Damascus also knows the world is new. Working within an apocalyptic framework, Paul calls Christ the Second Adam. His work will be as pervasive and effective as Adam's was pervasive and destructive. "For just as one man's disobedience made the mass of mankind sinners so this one's obedience will make the mass of them upright."[1] The early Fathers of the Church who loved a good image quickly seized on this one. A constant theme of Irenaeus stresses that if we fell through our solidarity with the First Man, we can be restored through our solidarity with Christ.

The title of Second Adam is probably the early Church's initial attempt at a Christian theology of history. Like all first Christian attempts, the Old Testament is its inspiration and guidance. The Hebrew concept of corporate personality underlies and gives validity to the designation of Christ as Second Adam. A corporate personality is a person in whom the values, ideals, and hopes of the entire group are summed up and expressed. In him and his activity the entire group (or race) either rises or falls. John McKenzie says this clearly and well: "Corporate personality means that a group is incorporated in the personality of its leader. The ancient king was the state and the nation. In him the people acted and suffered. His will was their will, his achievements their achievements, his failures their failures."[2]

In the first century Palestinian milieu Second Adam was undoubtedly a powerful image to communicate the new life of the risen Christ. But over the centuries it proved to have, as the sociologists would say, latent dysfunctions. It tended to objectify Christ, place redemption solely in a transpersonal order, and turn the Christian into a grandstand spectator. The Christian boos Adam who brought him to the sorry state he is in and cheers Christ who brings him out of it. In this context redemption becomes mechanistic and vague. Through the actions of Adam we automatically find ourselves in the situation of sin, of estrangement from God, self, and neighbor. So through the actions of Christ we should automatically find ourselves in the situation of justification, right relationship with God, self, and neighbor. The obvious and nagging question is: If Christ accomplished our redemption, where is it? Granted that we must have faith in him to receive the benefits of his work, it is still the handiwork of Adam more than the redemptive work of Christ which is our constant context. How exactly has Christ reversed Adam?

A greater difficulty arises for the concept of corporate personality when the historical existence of a single person named Adam is questioned. The word Adam in Hebrew signifies man in general. Adam as a definite, individual progenitor of the human race who committed certain acts which had lasting consequences did not exist. In fact, it is Paul Ricoeur's contention that only when the historicity of Adam as a single individual disappears will his monumental impact as a symbol emerge.[3] The story of Adam and his fall is a rendering of the existential situation of humankind. The story is not an historical explanation of human origins but an exploration of our enduring predicament. It is characteristic of the ancient mythic process to interpret the present situation by telling a story about how it began. In this way the Adam story, although intimately related to the human situation, is not a recording of a man and his wife and their tragic choice at the dawn of history. In contrast, the story of the Second Adam is historically grounded in the life of Jesus of Nazareth. The not inconsiderable difference is that the story of Adam is a timeless myth of human estrangement and the story of Christ, while a counter-myth of human communion, is warranted not because it is a valid ideal but because it occurred in a single, personal existence. The first and second Adams have radically different relationships to history.

Nevertheless, contrasting Adam and Christ can illuminate the processes of sin and redemption. However, they must not be treated as corporate personalities but as models of lived existence. The story of Adam portrays the lived existence of man in sin. The story of the Second Adam portrays the lived existence of man in grace. Redemption in terms of a transaction between supernatural powers, whether Christ overcoming Satan or Christ assuaging the Father, is the culture-bound theology of another age. Today the category which most effectively communicates the meaning of sin and redemption is lived existence. Sin is not an invisible mark on the soul but distorted personalities, twisted motives, oppressive and destructive lifestyles. Redemption is not an invisible slate wiped clean but liberated personalities, neighbor-centered motivation, life-styles which respect the freedom and well-being of every creature. Adam and Christ are two different models of lived existence, two different foundational ways of being-in-the-world. In Adam, the style of distrust and estrangement is symbolized. In Christ, the style of trust and communion is symbolized. Our age is impatient with the processes of mythologizing and unimpressed with the intricacies of philosophic logic. It returns again and again to the insistent question of lived existence: How is life enriched and how is it impoverished?

The story of Adam and Eve does not begin with

the snake but with the sixth day of creation when a jubilant but tired God entrusted the earth to their care and them to each other. Traditional theology has always stressed that creation was a totally gratuitous act of God. Everything that is is a gift from God and Genesis seems to imply that it is a gift given to humankind. God entrusts not only human existence but the entire earth to the gardener and his wife. It is in this context that "the most subtle of all the wild beasts"[4] slithers toward the woman with the question: "Did God really say you were not to eat from any of the trees in the garden?" The woman replies that they may eat of every tree but one tree. "And if we eat of that tree, we will be subject to death." The serpent says, "No! You will not die! God knows in fact that on the day you eat it your eyes will be opened and you will be like gods, knowing good from evil." This initial encounter with its deceptively simple dialogue explores the depth of the human predicament. The snake, to use the classic metaphor which implies growth and enlargement, sows the seeds of distrust. He subtly suggests that humankind's trust in God is ill-founded. The words of God's mouth do not match the thoughts of his mind and the feelings of his heart. He keeps Adam and Eve from the tree not because it will do them harm but because it will give them unbounded good. Humankind cannot trust God, for God will deceive them. In current jargon, it is a case of transference. The snake projects his own fork-tongued personality onto God and Adam and Eve choose to believe it. Enter the world of cosmic deceits, hidden agendas, treacherous motivations, illusions, and lies.

The snake's prediction is that Adam and Eve will be like gods. Instead they become less themselves. As open-ended creatures they fulfill themselves in acts of transcendence, the free centering of the self in God and the free movement outward toward the neighbor. This is why the snake's temptation is especially appealing. It promises permanent trans- cendence but what it delivers is permanent self- enclosure. By distrusting God they sever them- selves from the source and power to transcend. Adam and Eve settle within themselves and move from creaturely other-centeredness to idolatrous self-centeredness. Their basic relationship to exis- tence has been reversed. Once they dwelled within God's trust and returned that trust; they were free. Now they dwell in distrust which allows them only fear.

The moment Adam and Eve betray God's trust in them their trust in each other is broken. The Scrip- tures record the first effect of their free and alienat- ing act of distrust in God: "Then the eyes of both of them were opened and they realized that they were naked." They quickly sew fig leaves into clothes to hide their vulnerability. Nakedness has always been a symbol of trust. The nakedness of lovers says that each is willing to hand themselves over to the other. The trust is so deep and pervasive that they are able to venture all they are, their physical and psychic nakedness. Adam and Eve are suddenly aware they cannot take this risk. The religious dynamic has been set in motion. They cannot trust God so they cannot trust each other. Estrangement from the Ground of Being energized estrangement between beings. Enter the world of fear, alienation, manipulation, domination, and war.

The Adamic way of being-in-the-world has basically been established—distrust and estrangement. All that is needed is time for the devastating implications to work themselves out. Yahweh comes to the garden and Adam and Eve hide because they are naked. Yahweh asks, "Who told you you were naked?" Distrust of God, which always includes the betrayal of God's trust, told them they had to fear each other. But Adam was quick to the defense: "The woman whom you gave me made me do it." And Eve originated what would become the classic copout: "The devil made me do it." Enter the world of recrimination, injustice, scapegoating, and irresponsibility.

The story of Adam and Eve is not an interesting piece of history but a graphic representation of how we live. Its ancient framework is a religious faith which places high priority on humankind's relationship to God. The rupture of this relationship has repercussions throughout our personal and social life. Each person, although multidimensional, is a jealous unity which does not allow compartmentalization. Once humankind has replaced open allegiance to God with a fearful grip on their own selfhoods, the activities of life take a destructive turn. From the religious perspective we cannot be alienated from God and in creative communion with our neighbor. The source of our empowerment to be a person for others is that we are a person for God. The contemporary secular mood does not easily recognize estrangement from the last power of human life as the driving engine of our hostility toward each other. But what is becoming indisputable with all the power of survey empiricism is that the Adamic style of distrust and alienation dominates human interaction.

Although every period of history experiences the pains of estrangement, Robert Nesbet thinks our age is especially conscious of it. "It has become steadily clearer to me that alienation is one of those determining realities of the contemporary age. Not merely a key concept in philosophy, literature, and the social sciences—but a cultural and psychological condition implicating ever larger segments of the population."[5] This same radical awareness of alienation emerges in Nikos Kazantzakis' *The Odyssey: A Modern Sequel*. In Homer's epic, the battle weary Odysseus sets sail for Ithaca. For long years he fought in the Trojan war and now yearns for his homeland. Home is a primordial symbol of wholeness and peace. Home is where alienation gives way to togetherness, strangeness to familiarity, coldness to warmth. A homecoming, except in Harold Pinter's vicious play, is a time of joy. Conversely, invasion of the home is more than a crime; it is trespassing on the sacred. Odysseus values home so highly that he forsakes luxurious immortality with Calypso for Penelope and her needlepoint. Homer's epic ends in reconciliation. But when Kazantzakis begins his modern sequel, Odysseus' reconciliation becomes a new form of estrangement. No sooner has Odysseus slain the suitors than he realizes home will not cure his restlessness. Without looking back he deserts Ithaca and sets sail again. For the modern Odysseus home does not bring reconciliation but only an awareness of how deep his alienation is.

For most people, it is not literature and philosophy which convicts us of alienated life styles but the evening headlines. Despite the rhetoric of human solidarity and the agreed upon futility of war, conflicts erupt daily. Human estrangement is violently acted out in Indonesia, the Congo, the Sudan, Iraq, Cyprus, Palestine, Biafra, and Ulster. A modern parable points out the irony of this mutual distrust and its consequences.

> We began presumably with a nice village on the bank of a river. The only trouble was that down the river around the bend there was another village made up of people who were savages and barbarians. How did we know that? Why because they painted their faces blue and all civilized people like us painted their faces yellow. We thought about it for a while and realized that it was very likely those strangers were doubtlessly planning to attack us. Therefore we decided to attack them first. Sure enough halfway down the path on the river bank we encountered their way party coming to kill us.[6]

More personal forms of alienation are loneliness and conformity. David Riesmann in *The Lonely Crowd* argues that the alienated person is fast becoming a cultural type. It is not only that he has no sense of connectedness and rarely experiences satisfactory communication but he has developed an inner-isolation. He often remains unaffected by even violent encounters and has developed soul blindness—abnormally weak reactions to situations which should elicit strong emotion. The first line of Albert Camus' *The Stranger* is the classic example: "Mother died today. Or, maybe, yesterday; I can't be sure."[7] This is not solitude, time alone to reflect, but a hermetically sealed existence. Unfortunately, this state of lonely isolation is often unwittingly aggravated by the privacy Americans ardently seek. The other extreme is the "cheerful robot" described by C. Wright Mills. This person is not isolated from other people but submerged in them. He does not assert himself or make his own decisions. He is, in Heidegger's impersonal phrase, *das Man*, not an individual but the unthinking public.

The alienated life-style of American society could be endlessly elaborated. At one moment or another we have all thought we were Neil Simon's *Prisoner of Second Avenue*, heading for a personal nervous breakdown while the world was busy with a cosmic collapse. The religious insight into this situation suggests these proximate alienations are the outgrowth of an ultimate alienation. But simplicism must be guarded against. This does not mean reconciliation with God ends war, loneliness, conformity, violence, and hunger. The complex problems of political coalitions, interpersonal bargaining, and personal integration of myriad experiences are not automatically solved by reorienting ourselves with God. What religious intuition suggests is that these immediate alienations will only be aggravated until the foundational alienation is dealt with. Once ultimate distrust is in the process of being overcome or, to put it more positively, once ultimate trust is in the process of being established, people will gain the freedom to devise stratagems of successful reconciliation, to take the risk which will bring about community. This is not everything but it is the radical approach which religious people feel is necessary and which is too often overlooked.

The secret pain of the Adamic way of being-in-the-world is that the basic relationships are not destroyed but only severely distorted. Adam and Eve cannot dismiss God. They must relate to him but they will never again garden-stroll with him in the cool of the evening. Adam and Eve do not divorce. They stay together but now they stare at each other from their separate corners. Alienation is not total separation but dwelling wrongly in the complex of relationships which constitute historical life. At the center of alienation is an ache, a persistent pain for the way things should be. This may be expressed in the definite statement of G. K. Chesterton, "Whoever I am, I am not myself"[8] or in the pathetic wish of Andre Gide's character, "I should like to ring true."[9] With this understanding the Second Adam does not start over again. He does not create new givens for existence but appropriates what has always been in a salvific way. Theology expresses this insight by insisting that the Father of Jesus is the same God who created the world. The game is the same; only Jesus plays it differently. He dwells rightly within the relationships of God and neighbor. Entrusted by God, he returns trust to God. Entrusting his neighbors, he draws out their trustworthy selves. With his freedom, the First Adam became a stranger within creation; with his freedom, the Second Adam became its true citizen.

The B.B.C. production *Son of Man* begins in the Judean wilderness. A definitely middle-aged man is sprawled at the base of a desert dune. He is clawing at the sand in obvious psychic torment and his voice which is steadily rising and intensifying is dangerously near to the sing-song pattern of the insane: "Is it me? Is it me? Is it me?" At some unbearable interior peak the question is answered, his voice breaks and descends to a calm: "It is me. It is me. It is me." Although the B.B.C. portrayal of Jesus' vocational call is no more accurate than any other rendition, it emphasizes what is often overlooked. The crisis of faith for Jesus was not, at least in the first instant, whether God could be trusted. Although Yahweh's promises were often mysteriously fulfilled and it was never to be forgotten that "his ways are not our ways," the Jew generally took it for granted that God was trustworthy. The crisis for Jesus was to believe that God trusted him. The thrust of the satanic temptations is in the first word of the first clause: "*If* you are the son of God." Since when is God choosing the sons of carpenters to bring about his Kingdom? The Gospel summation of Jesus' vocational call does not come from the direction the modern mind expects. It is not the valiant affirmation of the earthbound Jesus, "There is a God and he cares" but the gracious affirmation of the heavenly Father: "You are my Beloved Son. On you my favor rests." This is the deepest meaning of the theological insistence that faith is a gift. The Kingdom has been handed over to us. We are entrusted with God, the universe, and our neighbor.

The trust of God in humankind is relentless. Yahweh's covenant agreement, "I am your God and you are my people," has no small print and is eternally binding. The escapades of Jonah is a comic book monument to the relentless trust of Yahweh. Yahweh singles out Jonah and entrusts him with the mission to preach repentance to the Ninevites. Jonah knows that the Ninevites are not partial to penitence and less than friendly to messengers of bad news. He decides to escape Yahweh's trust and books passage on the first boat out of Palestine. Once at sea, a fierce storm rocks the boat and the sailors know someone is a bad omen. Jonah is trying not to look guilty but he is soon on his way overboard. He sinks like a prophet to the bottom and a whale swallows him. After three days the whale swims to shore, belches him onto the beach, and the Lord God Yahweh says, "Now about Nineveh. . . ." The point is that not even at the bottom of the sea in the belly of a whale can you escape the relentless trust of God. The Old Testament is the story of a stiff-necked people pursued by an even stiffer-necked God.

In Jesus, God's relentless trust in humankind is relentlessly returned. Jesus hands himself and his life over to the purposes of God the way God hands himself over to the freedom of humankind. God is relentless because he will not abandon humankind. Jesus is relentless because he will not abandon the Kingdom. The enduring temptation throughout Jesus' ministry is to invest himself in something other than the Kingdom. Once Satan has failed to destroy Jesus' trust in God by tempting him to presume on it, he suggests a switch in allegiances—forsake God's Kingdom of suffering love and build a Jesus empire of power and wealth. Also Jesus' refusal to acknowledge titles or join existing power groups is dictated by the speciality of the Kingdom. He is scrupulous not to betray the Kingdom into Essene purity or Zealot nationalism or Temple law. Even the shrewd political advice not to go up to Jerusalem at the pasch is considered anti-Kingdom and so is called Satan, the seducer of God's plan. Jesus knows that to trust God means the hand is laid to the plow and the dead are left to bury the dead.

Jesus' trust in God was not a single decision which left him infallibly certain of his mission and God's support. The initial desert temptations of Satan were only round one. Angels might have come to minister to him but Luke said Satan "left him till another time."[10] It is admittedly guesswork (but not gratuitous guesswork) to surmise that Jesus went to the mountains to pray not because he was in lockstep toward the Kingdom but because he had to recommit his freedom to the trust God had given him. That there were second thoughts, anguish, and all-out doubt is revealed in the Gethsemane agony. "Abba, all things are possible to thee. Take this cup away from me yet not what I will but what you will."[11] The same Jesus who Luke says sweats blood, cries out on the cross, "My God, my God, why have you forsaken me?"[12] These are the opening words of Psalm 21, the cry of the desolate spirit. But the psalm which begins in abandonment and doubt ends in affirmation and conviction.

> The whole earth, from end to end, will remember and come back to Yahweh;
> all the families of the nations will bow down before him.
> For Yahweh reigns, the ruler of nations!
> Before him all the prosperous of the earth will bow down,
> before him will bow all who go down to the dust.
> And my soul will live for him, my children will serve him;
> men will proclaim the Lord to generations still to come,
> his righteousness to a people yet unborn. All this he has done.[13]

God raises Jesus from the dead not because he never flinched, talked back, or questioned but having flinched, talked back, and questioned he remained faithful.

God proclaimed his trust in Jesus at his baptism by calling him Son. Jesus symbolizes his returning trust in God by calling him Abba (Father). It has been suggested that the closest English equivalent of Abba is Daddy. Abba is a term which denotes special intimacy and tenderness. Against the background of a Judaism in which some factions would not even speak the name of God for fear of profaning it, calling God Abba is a scandal and a shock. Jesus seemed to have little reverence in the traditional temple sense. When the disciples asked Jesus to teach them how to pray, the first word he utters is Abba. The rest of the Lord's prayer unpacks the profound meaning of this word. Yet not everyone is

bold enough to call God Abba. Only those who
have experienced and responded to the Kingdom
say Abba because this word expresses the meaning
of their restructured lives. Abba is one of those
words directly traceable to the historical Jesus and
so has a special place in the Christian's vocabulary.

In contemporary society, Father symbolism is
under attack from many sides. The most straight-
forward charge is that when God is Father, humankind is relegated to an eternal childhood. Jesus'
saying, "Unless you become like a little child, you
shall not enter into the Kingdom of God"[14] merges
with his Father symbolism to irk humankind-
come-of-age. In this symbolism humankind never
grows up. We are always dependent, waiting for
inspiration, direction and permission. The Fatherhood of God may be the logical, symbolic base for
the family of man but it suppresses human adulthood. The best we can do in this symbolism is
endlessly petition a sugar-daddy deity.

Through psychoanalytic concepts this argument
is slickly extended into the Oedipus complex. In
modern times the symbol of God the Father moves
unwittingly into the Freudian arena of sexual
jealousy, patricide, and guilt. Even if the symbol of
Father does not call forth the full range of attitudes
and emotions which energize the Oedipus myth, it
definitely brings to mind the core of the myth
—rebellion of the son against the father. The son's
destiny is to overthrow the father and obtain his
rights and privileges. The relationship of the father
and son is ambivalent, marked by love and fear,
respect and guilt, obedience and rebellion. Religi-

ous ritual becomes a complex system of handling these oscillating feelings. In contemporary society, the symbol of Father attracts meanings which invalidate it as an expression of the God-humankind relationship.

A third and more recently mounted attack unmasks Father symbolism as ideology. The argument runs: If the heavenly God is a Father who oversees his sons and daughters on earth, then it is in the nature of things that society be male-dominated. The symbol of the Father reflects a patriarchal bias, bolsters the false consciousness of male supremacy, and legitimates the second-citizenry of women. The ideological underpinnings of the symbol for God must not be those of suppression and dominance but those of liberation and equality.

These shortcomings of Father symbolism which contemporary society quickly recognizes are definitely real but do not apply to the Abba of Jesus. Jesus' relationship to Abba does not make him a dependent child but a free, action-oriented adult. Abba is not a patriarch jealously guarding his prerogatives and suppressing the initiative of his sons and daughters. Abba is Father but what he fathers is the possibility of new life. He relates not to the bondage of childhood but to the hope of true adulthood. To focus on the biological and kinship elements of the symbol of Father is often misleading. There is nothing genetic or dutiful about the relationship. God's relationship to humankind becomes a Father's to his children only by mutual adoption. The only way that God is Father is if he is freely chosen; the only way humankind is child is if they are freely chosen. With this emphasis on the element of freedom the symbol slowly moves from Father-patriarch to Father-friend. Father-friend may be a potent symbol in a society where longevity demands parent-child relationships be restructured along parent-adult child-adult lines. If God is the ground of personal life and to be symbolized as a person, a sex must be chosen. Admittedly to call God an androgyne is middle ground but it is the flippant suggestion of the mythologically educated.[15] Every symbol has leanings and Fatherhood obviously leans towards masculine priorities. But a symbol only becomes a full-blown ideology when used with malice aforethought. In the hands of the insecure and dominating, every sumbol is a weapon. Abba is the symbol of Jesus and the linguistic center of the community he founded. If it has become ideological, it should be purged but not jettisoned. Abba is the Christian symbol for the ultimate power of human life, whom we trust and who trusts us with the future of the earth and our neighbor.

The Second Adam is the lived existence of Jesus of Nazareth which reestablishes the bonds of trust between God and humankind. The Jesus who claims God is Father reflects this relationship outward into the affairs of humankind. He who is entrusted and who trusts in God acts as God's representative and entrusts others and elicits trust from them. This is the foundational ethical principle of Jesus—give to others what you have received from God. The parable which most pointedly states this principle is the Unmerciful Servant. The servant is chastized because he did not "imitate the reality he had known."[16] He was forgiven a nine million dollar debt but did not forgive a fifteen dollar debt. He has betrayed God's forgiveness by not reflecting it outward toward his fellowperson. What he failed to understand is that response to God's love is not gratitude but imitation.

The Jesus who is entrusted by God entrusts those whom he encounters. The most notable example of Jesus trusting another is the man who in the New Testament symbolizes the Church—Peter. In the interactions of Jesus and Peter it is difficult to tell which incidents have a historical base and which are solely a theological lesson. Yet, for our purposes, the basic contours of the relationship are discernible. In the Gospel of John, Jesus meets Simon for the first time and dubs him the Rock. Jesus is immediately entrusting him and eliciting from him fidelity to that trust. This is not subtle gamesmanship and over-expectation which immediately throws a person off balance and eventually induces guilt. It is a call to all Peter is, which is obviously much more than he knows. Of course, it is the timeless theme of preachers that Simon the Rock proves no such thing. He grumbles about Jesus' nonsensical fishing instructions and then is overcome with guilt at the miraculous catch. He thinks Jesus' death too high a price to pay for fidelity to Kingdom and is rebuked as Satan. He forbids the Master to wash his feet; but on finding out it is this or nothing, he impetuously wants his head and hands bathed also. In the hour of crisis his hick

Galilean accent gives him away but he saves himself by denying the man he promised, "I would be
ready to go to prison with you, and to death."[17]
Peter's hesitant and vacillating responses to Jesus
culminate in denial. But in the Gospel of John, the
risen Christ does not match rejection with rejection.
He three times asks Peter if he loves him. After each
"yes" Peter is commissioned to feed the sheep.
Jesus is pursuing Peter into the center of his guilt
and calling him out of it. He is entrusting him who
proved trustless with the leadership of the community. The Son of the God of Israel is as relentless
as his Father.

The challenge of Jesus to trust is to know oneself
as entrusted and to entrust others. This is obviously
far from the conventional meaning of trust as a
passive handing over of responsibility. It is an active empowerment of others to be everything they
can be. The betrayal of trust is not so much the
betrayal of the person who trusts but of the self
which accepted the trust and then betrayed it. Undoubtedly, Jesus suffered knowing that Peter denied him but Peter himself was shattered: "And he
went out and wept bitterly."[18] The Gospel story of
the hanged Judas implies that he knew he destroyed himself in the act of betraying another. To
trust someone is to call to their better self to act in a
new way. When the call is not answered, the self
recedes into its own dark, narcissistic depths. In
this context, relentless trust is the Christian process
of conversion. It is the over and over again appeal to human freedom, the work of the importun-
ing God who will not break down the door but then

again will not stop knocking. There is no arm-
bending or coercion, just the continual solicitation
of human generosity which trust intuits to be there.
From this perspective, the idea of a totally depraved
humankind (a theme which will be explored in the
next chapter) is a blasphemy for it persists in thinking us worse than God does. Relentless trust knows
humankind is intractable but its deeper intuition is
that persisted-in love will not go unresponded to.

For the suspicious person (which is each one of
us) to talk of trusting others is to remember the
hucksterism of P. T. Barnum: "There is a sucker
born every minute and two to take him." Trust does
not mean gullibility. It is not blind to evil and deception but it does not allow them to dictate the
terms of the relationship. Gratuitous trust attempts
to overcome negative and destructive situations by
evoking trust from the other. Non-violent resistance is an example of an attempt at radically redemptive trust. Gandhi insists on trust even in situations where the opponent is likely to betray it: "A
Satyagrahi bids goodby to fear. He is never afraid to
trust the opponent. Even if the opponent plays him
false twenty times, the Satyagrahi is ready to trust
him the twenty-first time, for an implicit trust in
human nature is the very essence of his creed."[19]
The twenty-first time of Hindu trust closely resem-
bles the seventy-times-seven times that a Christian
must forgive his fellowperson. The "implicit trust
in human nature" of Gandhi also has a Christian
parallel in the Quaker notion of "answering that of
God in every man." If the Christian is God-like, it
will penetrate to the God in every person and evoke

a response, hopefully conversion. The redemptive entrusting which pacifism attempts appears to most people as foolhardy and unproductive. Yet it has the type of abandon and neighbor-centeredness which is the distinctive style of Jesus.

A more moderate outlook on entrusting others and one which is more readily espoused is stated by Seward Hiltner:

> 1. As a realist I know that the world is a rough place, and I shall not be shattered or disillusioned when I find untrustworthiness just where I have least expected it. But the world is also full of potentialities, and I shall not permit my awareness of untrustworthiness to shield my perception away from serious pursuit of those potentials. . . .
>
> 3. Even though most of life declares its ambiguity in capital letters, I know nevertheless that I have experienced great moments when the unambiguous, the wholly trustworthy, has been a part of my experience. I resolve not to become so suspicious that I shall fail to recognize such gifts, no matter where they may come from. On the other side, I pledge that I shall not concentrate so hard on grail-hunting that I shall distort the ambiguities that make up most of my experience.
>
> 4. I have no apology for a prudent suspicion that tests out whatever or whoever claims to be trustworthy. But I shall permit this attitude to occupy only a preliminary place in my relationships. With persons I like, such an attitude soon disappears. But even with those I do not like or cannot understand, I shall endeavor to remain open to anything in the other that is worthy of trust.
>
> 5. If I can maintain this attitude of paradox, yet with a slant always in the direction of readiness to trust wherever there are partially trustworthy elements, then I shall feel that I am responding to something in the creation itself but in no way being forced or compelled.[20]

The extent and effectiveness of trust is an important but endless discussion. What can be asserted here is the centrality of trust in the message and life of Jesus.

The Christian entrusts others because he has been entrusted by God and he trusts in God. Trust in God who is the Abba of Jesus must be sharply distinguished from reliance, security, and presumption. Reliance carries the connotation not only of handing over to another but also of dumping responsibility. "I am relying on you" translates to "You do it." Relying on God in the sense that He will do what I cannot do is abdicating Christian identity which is precisely to do what God wants done. False security is an attempt to stop the world. It cannot bear not to be in control—safety is its only passion. Trust in God is not this type of security but the power to live creatively in a fundamentally ambiguous and unmanageable existence. Presumption is the most insidious and debilitating of religious attitudes. It ceaselessly and secretly expects God to intervene in human affairs. Presumption leaps from the pinnacle of the temple and expects to float down; says "Lord, Lord," and expects cancer to go away; does not provide food but expects manna to fall from heaven. The theological arguments which support an interventionary God are many and varied and people daily say God has cured them. Yet one brutal historical fact remains—Jesus is mercilessly nailed to the cross and despite the Matthean boast, twelve legions of angels did not save him from that hour. No cop-out redemption theories that say God wanted it that way explain the lonely and unvisited death of God's Son. This side of the grave Jesus is left totally unvalidated by the Lord of heaven and earth. Trust in God does not presume that God will intervene.

If false reliance, security, and presumption were eliminated the effects on Christian life style would be immeasurable. This is the theme of a long but insightful paragraph in Leander Keck's *A Future For The Historical Jesus:*

> In this light, the vindication of Jesus—the Jesus whose life does not end with manifest proof of his validity—means that he who restructures his understanding of God and of himself on the basis of Jesus can come to terms with his own incompleteness, with the non-validated character of his own existence. He is freed from the compulsion of vindicating himself or knowing that others do so, and from the demand that God vindicate him now. Instead, on the basis of Jesus he ventures to entrust himself and his vindication to God, and is prepared to receive it where Jesus did—beyond death. Thereby he is reconciled to his own unfinishedness and mortality, and to the One whom he trusts to affirm him beyond the night of death. Such a theological understanding underlies Jesus' own words about the secret righteousness that depends totally on God alone for vindication (Mt. 6:1-18), and lays hold of Paul's insight that on the basis of Jesus one ceases to establish his own righteousness but relies on God's verdict. Further, he who trusts God on this basis is liberated also from the compulsion to prove the Christian hope to be correct by historical progress, but knows that he can live in a world of broken hopes without himself being broken because the event of Jesus has taught him that God's relation to him and the world cannot be inferred directly from man's attainments. Armed with this freedom, he is also free to change the

world, for on the one hand, this world does not legitimate him any longer, and, on the other, he knows that whatever happens to him cannot really separate him from God because nothing finally separated Jesus from God either.[21]

In extreme situations, trust in God comes down to the saying of the much afflicted yet stubborn Job: "Even though he slay me, I will trust in him."

The struggle which characterizes Christian life is symbolized by the clashing facts that we are both sons of Adam and heirs of Christ. The Adamic way of distrust and estrangement is all too easy. We seem programmed to jump back from the limits of life and to hold the self in such reserve that we are inhibited from reaching toward our neighbor. The Christic way of trust and communion demands courage. It is responding to the God who trusts us and in whom we trust by creating a community of mutual entrustment. Only radical faith can bring the joyous freedom necessary to carry out this project. What John says about the self-understanding and daring action of the Second Adam could never be said about the First Adam:

> Jesus knew that the Father had *entrusted* everything into his hands, and that he had come from God and was returning to God, and he got up from table, removed his outer garment and, taking a towel, wrapped it round his waist; he then poured water into a basin and began to wash the disciples' feet and to wipe them with the towel he was wearing.[22]

Chapter 6

The Challenge To Forgive

It is the stubborn yet unrecognized fact that forgiveness, as it is currently preached, has no impact because people just do not think they are all that bad. Of course no one will deny being a sinner but few would go along with Martin Luther's masochistic evaluation, "I am dust and ashes and full of sin."[1] If asked whether humankind is basically good or evil, Christians, trained to the teeth, will parrot evil. But having said it and being willing to defend it, they behave as if people basically leaned toward goodness.

To return to the theme of the last chapter, most people's fundamental stance toward others, even strangers, is trustful. If a person stops us on the street to ask the time of day, we give him the benefit of the doubt that the hour is what he is after and not our money. Until the person has proven himself treacherous, we presume him trustworthy. This is, of course, a petty example and the person who wishes to stress human iniquity can cite the twentieth century replete with gas ovens and napalm as proof. But to attribute the horrors people inflict on each other and on the earth to their core wickedness may be too quick. The prevalence of evil may not indicate total depravity but the ease with which human goodness gets corrupted.

If an average Christian would foolhardily suggest that his sinfulness is set in the larger context of his goodness, the preacher's kneejerk reaction would be, "Oh no it isn't." To this might be added the condescension that this person's self-image is naive and he has not fathomed the unfathomable depth of his own evil. Sin is not something we do but something we are. Bonhoeffer criticizes existential theologians because they drag basically balanced people to an open grave and make them stare into it till they feel dread. This pre-evangelization gimmick is supposed to ready them for the good news. In the same way, the acknowledgment of our sinfulness is the traditional springboard to the acknowledgment of God's grace. Luther's injunction, "pecca fortiter" (sin mightily) is built on the premise that the experience of personal wickedness is the concomitant of the experience of God's grace. When the well-scrubbed student from Moody Bible Institute confronts the passenger on the bus with, "Are you saved?" what he means is, "Do you experience yourself as a forgiven sinner?" To that question only a few contemporary Christians would respond "Yes, but much more than that. I experience myself as a good person who when frightened or hurt or under pressure acts unjustly and inhumanly toward my neighbor. But with the help of God's grace and my freedom, what is good in me will overcome what is evil."

This Christian response raises many traditional theological problems and threatens certain renditions of the gratuity of grace. Has Pelagius returned with tennis shorts and racket to proclaim the sufficiency of natural man? To say God loves us even though we are sinners is to breathe a sigh of relief. We were afraid that our incessant bumbling and deliberate malice might exclude us from human fulfillment. We are eternally (literally) grateful to this God for his free and undeserved love and we will remember to pray to and praise so large-hearted a benefactor. With this piety the Christian rhapsodizes over a God who so magnanimously forgives and loves. But what kind of love focuses so exclusively on forgiving or, in some theologies, overlooking? Is it not possible that God, even knowing the mean little longings of our mean little hearts, spies a generosity that he is passionately attracted to? Humankind cannot be so undesirable if God has panted after us since the beginning. That humankind is a marred beauty, a wrongheaded energy, and a deceptive truth is not to be argued. But perhaps what urges God on is the beauty, energy, and truth and not the mar, wrongheadedness, and deception. The fact that humankind has positive and attractive qualities does not mean we have a claim on God's love. God's love is still a free bestowal of himself which enables humankind to act courageously. But it might be well to shift the emphasis from "in spite of the fact we are sinners" to "because of the fact that we are lovable."

Forgiveness in the context of human sinfulness is a vastly different dynamic than forgiveness in the context of human goodness. In the context of human sinfulness forgiveness is easily perverted. The unalterable fact is that someone is always on the top and someone is always on the bottom. The penitent comes, hat in hand and sin in heart, to say, "Sorry." He is the sinner and, within the rules of the forgiveness game, at a decided disadvantage. For the moment, wrong is the whole story about him and the only thing that will put him right is pain equal to and sometimes exceeding the pain he has caused. Obsequiousness and grovelling are splendid forms of self-abasement and sufficient suffering to even the score. In most cases the sinner takes his sin with a grain of salt and is not all that sorry. But the liturgy of forgiveness, which forbids spontaneity and insures the playing of wooden roles, demands a long face, halting speech, firm purpose of amendment, and almost-held-back tears. This stylized ritual is humiliating to the penitent but once forgiveness is given he is too busy feeling relieved to reflect on it.

The forgiveness game which does not respect the penitent seduces the forgiver into a more subtle perversion. There is seductive power to the Keys of the Kingdom. To remit sin and graciously bestow relief and happiness or to retain sin and watch the person squirm in guilt—which shall it be, my Lord? Also, forgiveness can turn into domination, a conquering act which burns the sin into the forehead of the penitent. Forgiveness does not do away with sin but psychologically insists on it.

These underlying yet controlling feelings of penitent and forgiver are sharply handled in a scene from one of P. G. Wodehouse's novels:

> It is a good rule in life never to apologize. The right sort of people do not want apologies and the wrong sort take a mean advantage of them. Sellers belonged to the latter class. When Annette, meek, penitent, with all her claws sheathed came to him and grovelled, he forgave her with a repulsive magnanimity which in a less subdued mood would have stung her to renewed pugnacity. As it was, she allowed herself to be forgiven and retired with a dismal conviction that from now on he would be more insufferable than ever.[2]

Annette and Sellers have no respect for each other but out of social politeness and inner guilt they play the forgiveness game.

This type of forgiveness, which dotes on human sinfulness, encourages the worst in everybody. A cynic might conclude that every act of forgiveness is a new sin. The sinful behavior which separates two people becomes a weapon which both wield out of their psychological needs and for their interpersonal advantage. This is far from the forgiveness process which Jesus envisioned. The forgiveness of God which Jesus proclaims and which he urges humankind to imitate does not focus on sin but is a direct appeal to human goodness. To understand forgiveness in the context of human goodness it is necessary to explore the central symbol of Jesus' personality and mission—the Kingdom of God.

There is only one thought in the mind of Jesus, only one feeling in his heart, only one cry in his mouth—the Kingdom of God. Of all the titles given to Jesus and the honors accorded him, the most accurate historically is that he is the Proclaimer of the Kingdom. In contemporary culture, the symbol of the Kingdom of God has no cash value. It does not mobilize feelings and it takes extensive explanation to even begin to understand its meaning. But in the Hebrew world of Jesus, the Kingdom of God was a fire-phrase. Heads turned in instant recognition; avid conversations followed; conspiracies were founded. Like all central and powerful symbols, the Kingdom of God generated many interpretations. Messianic pretenders used the Kingdom as a rallying cry for a revolt against Rome. They wished to hurry the Kingdom along by starting wars which they hoped God would finish. The National Liberation Front of ancient Palestine were the Zealots. Most likely the Roman state sentenced Jesus to death because they mistook him for a Zealot. Galilee was Zealot territory and any person coming out of Galilee and preaching the Kingdom was immediately suspect. Although evidence was certainly lacking to prove Jesus an insurrectionist, his unpopularity with the Jewish leaders insured there would be no outcry if Rome took preventative action. The exact facts of the trial and death of Jesus are hotly disputed, especially between Christians and Jews. In fact, a few years ago an Israeli lawyer wanted to reopen the case in light of new evidence. The religious conflicts Jesus engaged in certainly pushed him towards the cross. He said, "Love your enemies," when in order to survive the Jews had to hate theirs. But it is chilling to note that at least a supporting reason for his death was the blind, unyielding prejudice that has crucified so many—the accident of his birth. He was a Galilean and therefore a violent insurrectionist. The argument whether Jew or Roman is responsible for Jesus' death must be relaxed by the theological insistence that the Christ-killer is sin.

The Kingdom of God which Jesus proclaimed was less pretentious than violent revolution. When the Pharisees asked Jesus when the Kingdom was coming he replied, "The Kingdom is not coming with signs to be observed; nor will they say, 'Lo here it is!' or 'There', for behold, the Kingdom of God is in the midst of you."[3] Jesus cautions against the spectacular. The Kingdom does not come like Roman legions whose dust can be seen in the distance and whose approach can be calculated nor does it come on the clouds in a cataclysmic setting. (This has to be balanced with the general apocalyptic leanings of Jesus.) The Kingdom is not a thing to be observed but the experience of God within human activity. Through Jesus' words and deeds the experience of the Kingdom is present and active. Its fullness, when God will be all in all and humankind will be at peace, is in the future.

The follower of Jesus lives between the already and not yet of the Kingdom of God. The present experience of the Kingdom is both an anticipation and guarantee of future fulfillment. Jesus does not spell out this future hope in terms of date and hour. In this he seems to have departed radically from his contemporaries and some of ours who revel in setting dates for the end of the world and repairing to the nearest mountaintop. Jesus' idea of time does not emphasize the concept of succeeding moments.

To Jesus, time is opportunity. To talk of the future is a way to free the present moment for decision and action. Do not shade your eyes and peer into the distance for the first sight of the Kingdom of God. It is among us now, challenging our presuppositions and actions.

The Kingdom of God which is among us is not manifested in the parting of the sea or the calling down of fire from heaven but in the forgiveness of sins. To experience the God of Jesus is to experience yourself as forgiven. The forgiveness of God does not dialogue and debate with sin but cuts through it to confront human goodness. This style of forgiving is revealed in the parable of the Wastrel Son and in Jesus' interaction with Zacchaeus.

The young Wastrel, having squandered his inheritance, is stranded in a foreign land tending swine. The picture could not be more dismal. For a Jew to live among Gentiles meant constant defilement but to tend his swine was an abomination. It is sheer hunger which brings the son to his senses and he begins his journey toward home and food. He will not ask his father for the privileges of sonship—he has squandered them forever—but only to be taken on as a hired hand. The son expects a forgiveness which will concentrate on his sin and exploit his shame. As a mere hired hand on the family farm his sin would be forever with him, his guilt there every day for all to see. At this point the listener might agree with the son's modest job request and take a "serves him right" attitude. The next sentence however is a startling scene. "While he was still a long way off, his father saw him and was moved with pity. He ran to the boy, clasped him in his arms and kissed him tenderly."[4] Joachim Jeremias says that running is "a most unusual and undignified procedure for an aged oriental."[5] It seems Abba, much like his son Jesus, does not stand on protocol. The son asks only for a job but the father will have none of it. Instead of making him a servant he tells the servants, "Quick! Bring out the best robe and put it on him; put a ring on his finger and sandals on his feet. Bring the calf we have been fattening, and kill it; we are going to have a feast, a celebration, because this son of mine was dead and has come back to life; he was lost and is found." And they began to celebrate.[6] The Father's forgiveness is not just a putdown of the son which reduces him to a servant but a reaffirmation of his worth as a son. The party celebrates not the return of the sinner, as the older brother insists, but the return of the good son who had so long been eclipsed by sin. This difference is not merely word play but reveals a deep conviction about humankind.

A dwarfish but self-important tax collector hanging from the limb of a tree in order to catch a glimpse of a passing prophet is obviously looking for something.[7] Jesus confronts Zacchaeus with neither outrage nor condescension. He does not berate him for living off the blood money of his own people nor pat him on the head and agree that he is a worthless and pitiful character. Instead, Jesus invites himself to dinner. To modern ears, Jesus' self-invitation is rude and presumptuous. But in the context of Palestinian custom this gesture is an acceptance of Zacchaeus. For the Hebrew the meal is a sacred action. To share bread with another is to affirm that person in your sight and in the sight of God. That is why Zacchaeus is startled when it is his despised and much-rejected house that Jesus chooses. Zacchaeus knows that Jesus is not approving his cheating and graft but his fundamental created self-worth. The meal says "Zacchaeus, this heartless thievery is not you. You are more than this." Jesus does not pound home his sin but calls to his goodness. Zacchaeus responds to who he really is, a created son of the Father, repents, and leads a new life. Forgiveness is not magnanimously forgetting faults but the uncovering of self-worth when it is crusted over with self-hatred.

This style of forgiving in both God and Jesus is what Richard Ray calls "appreciative grace." Sheer grace is an indiscriminate dumping of mercy on everything in sight. The graciousness of God focuses exclusively on the fact that although nobody deserves it, everybody gets it. Appreciative grace is rooted in the doctrine that all creation is good and therefore takes into account the attractiveness and worth of the person. Appreciative grace suggests a new interpretation and style of forgiving. Sin does not destroy the relationship between God and humankind. As was mentioned before, alienation presupposes that the relationship endures but in a distorted form. This is the thrust of the classic distinction between human nature as deprived or depraved. Deprived human nature is good but fallen; depraved human nature is fallen. In the context of appreciative grace and deprived human nature, forgiveness reclaims the essential worth of the person. It is rooted in a love which is faithful to the true self of the neighbor and continues to call to it. Ray says it well:

> Forgiveness can be described in interpersonal terms as the reaffirmation of the essential worth of one who has become blind to, and insensitive of, his own sense of worth. It includes the experience of being embraced for *who one really is*. Forgiveness is thus an experience of insight which comes with the aid of another whose vision has not been distorted to such a degree. Thus, forgiveness is not so much an act of mercy as it is an act of loyalty to truth. Truth, not mercy, is the source from which one's self-respect is renewed and confidence and hope restored. Forgiveness can also be described as a celebration of the worth of one or more persons in particular, and of human nature in general. It is a celebration in which the transgressor and the transgressed both participate. In this dimension it is also an ecstasy; it is a pause in which the transgressor and the transgressed share in a new recognition of the worth of each. In metaphysical terms, forgiveness is the revival of consonance with the structures of personal existence.[8]

The experience of forgiveness which Jesus proclaims is a possibility for humankind not because we are a sinful people but because we are good people who sin.

Although the forgiveness of God mediated through Jesus is primarily an experience of the individual, it has definite reverberations in the social order. In Hebrew society, sin was not the isolated, trivial, and patronized concept it is today. Sin intertwined with race and wealth was the controlling factor in determining social position. It formed the boundaries between classes and distinguished the prestigious from the infamous, the accepted from the rejected. For the Jews, society had a basic threefold sin-oriented division.[9]

First there was the good Jew. Although he was a sinner, his fundamental option (to use a current concept) was the path of the Lord. When the coming Kingdom arrived, he would be welcomed into it with humility and joy. The second category was the Gentile. The Gentile's allegiances were not in line with the true God and so he was confirmed in sin. Even so, when the Kingdom came, there was some hope, very slight, that the exceptionally virtuous Gentile would find a home. The third category, the significant one for understanding Jesus' ministry, is the Jew who had made himself a Gentile. For this person there was almost no hope. When the Kingdom came, he would be among those on the outside weeping and gnashing their teeth. The Jew who had made himself a Gentile had betrayed his sacred heritage and nothing was more despicable and damning. A Jew could become a Gentile by being a tax collector, murderer, extortionist, or even a swineherd. The radical message of the parable of the Wastrel Son is not fully understood until it is realized the Father is welcoming back he who fell among the swine, a Jew who had made himself a Gentile. For the Jew, the primary factor in class stratification was not blood or wealth but the extent of sinfulness.

This social structure in interaction with the fact that Palestine was the occupied territory of the

Roman empire formed the socio-political environment of Jesus. In the context of Hebrew history, the invasion of Rome only meant that once again the Jews would resist any intermingling with their Gentile conquerors and harden their hearts with righteous disdain. To maintain their identity they would close ranks and present a solid wall of defiance. This Jewish attitude towards Roman occupation creeps into the trial accounts in the Gospel of John. Even when they wished Pilate to do them the favor of sentencing Jesus to death, they would not enter his house and be defiled. [10] In this political climate, tax collectors are the despicable people who have gone over to the enemy. They are collaborators who are profiting from the humiliation of their people. This is the socio-political context for the distinctive feature of Jesus' ministry—table fellowship. The ultimate charge of the Pharisees was that Jesus was a "glutton and a drunkard, a friend of tax collectors and sinners." His enacted parable of table fellowship is more scandalous and dangerous than any of his spoken parables. To the sharp eyes of the Jewish leaders this symbol of God's forgiveness goes beyond personal metanoia to threaten the religious, social, and political status quo.

The immediate and almost unthinkable implication of Jesus' table fellowship is that the Jews have been wrong about God. God does not reject the sinner and pull the righteous to his bosom. He is not a Lord of sharp delineations but of open, ever-welcoming embrace. Jesus' answer to those respectable people who ask why he associates with riff-raff and scum is paraphrased by Joachim Jeremias:

> Because they are sick, and need me, because they are truly repentant, and because they feel the gratitude of children forgiven by God; and because you, with your loveless, selfrighteous, disobedient hearts, reject the gospel. But above all, because God is like that, so kind to the poor, so glad when the lost are found, so full of a father's love for the child who has gone wrong, so merciful to the despairing, the helpless, and the needy. That is why![11]

This new religious reality which Jesus preaches has sociopolitical connotations. Jesus proclaims that table fellowship with Gentiles and Jews who have made themselves Gentiles is not betrayal of God's kingdom but a sign of its coming. Does this mean then that Israel is to welcome those who betrayed and oppressed her? What will become of a small people if they make overtures of welcome to their enemies? They will disappear in persecution and intermarriage. The promise of Abraham to make his seed as numberless as the stars of the sky and the sand of the sea will be void. It might have been thinking like this that urged the Johannine high priest to say, "It is better that one man die than the whole people perish."[12]

The forgiving Father of Jesus may bring personal hope and redemption but he also challenges the existing socio-political structure. If the forgiveness of God cuts through sinful action and goes beyond it to elicit each person's created goodness, the power of a society which exploits the sin situation is broken. This is the social meaning of interpreting Jesus as God's warrior in deadly combat with Satan for the possession of humankind. In the Gospel stories the demons who possess people immediately recognize Jesus for who he is, the exorcising finger of God and their mortal enemy. When Jesus drives out demons, it is more than a personal eviction notice. It is the social message that evil no longer has the power to distort human relationships. That Jesus breaks the rule of Satan means that sin and the social structure which reflects and reinforces sin should not continue to dominate us.

What the radical forgiveness of God means to Jesus is that communities are not built on blood or wealth or righteousness but on creaturehood. To sit at the table with Jesus one does not have to be ritually pure or socially approved or economically well-off. All that is required is that the person had experienced the forgiveness of sins and reaffirmed his creaturehood under the Fatherhood of God. The practical consequence of this is that one never knows who one will be eating with. Since every person is creature and capable of being stunned into conversion, the Christian community is, to say the least, an interesting mix. The whore down the street becomes your sister in faith. The Roman soldier who occupies your country now shares your cup. The tax collector, who, on the first of the month, never forgets to knock on your door, breaks bread with you. Biological kinships, as precious and meaningful as they are, are engulfed by this religious reality and the new answer to the simple question, "Who is my mother and brother and sister?" becomes the person who hears the Word of

God and keeps it.

At first glance, this community gathered around Jesus seems an indiscriminate lot—the wealthy Joseph of Arimathea hobnobbing with Mary Magdalene—but this is not the case. The party which Jesus throws has a very selective guest list but the basis of the selection is not the traditional one. Only creatures are invited. To all those who insist on being god, who will not abandon their manufactured superiority, the door is closed. The only "Open Sesame" is the experience of the forgiveness of sin which is the experience of the freedom and goodness of human creaturehood. Then the door is opened, not begrudgingly but joyfully, for God is the Father of all creatures and you were truly missed at his Feast of Life. The experience of forgiveness is the wedding garment for the banquet of Jesus. Note that it is a wedding garment, the robe of joy and communion, not sack-cloth and ashes, the sign of the sinner. This wedding garment cannot be purchased with money or blue blood or the purest intention because it is the free gift of the Father to those who acknowledge him. To those who have bought heavily into the social structure based on alienation, the community of Jesus may be disconcerting—just as it is disconcerting that the Samaritan rather than the Jew proved neighbor, that the Publican rather than the Pharisee went home justified, that the beautiful people who were invited do not come and the dispossessed of the highways and byways enter the feast—but it is not indiscriminate.

The Church has always had to struggle to keep

forgiveness of sin and the later coordinate, the baptismal experience of dying and rising with Christ, the only criterion for membership in the Christian community. At the very beginning of the Church a faction called the Judaizers wanted to add requirements. A Gentile who wanted to become a Christian had to pass through Judaism. Besides entering into the Christ event and being reborn he had to enter into the Abraham event and be circumcised. This position was defeated at the Council of Jerusalem in 51 but the temptation lingered and was more successful in later Church history. When the Church became synonymous with Western civilization, the entrance into the community of Christ meant that one had to adopt, in various ways, Latin customs. The whole background of the odious phrase "Christian colonialism" is that the Church demanded more than creaturehood and imposed more than the free invitation of Jesus. Whenever this happens the power and uniqueness of Jesus' community is dissolved. A community built on what alienates us from each other is not redemptive but another example of the ease and seductiveness of sin. The religious reality of forgiveness which Jesus preached and the community of creaturehood he gathered around himself is as radical a challenge in the 1970s as it was two thousand years ago.

To say that the community of Jesus is built on the radical recognition of creaturehood is not to deny the diversity of talents among its members. Each person's uniqueness and ability is acknowledged but what is relished beyond all else is the common gift of creaturehood. The foundation of Jesus' community is the question of, to use the Pauline phrase, what are we to glory in? If talent or inheritance or success are gloried in, they become, even though they may not be acknowledged, the existential foundation of the community. Those who follow Jesus glory in the fact that they are sons and daughters of the Father. This creaturehood base for community is paradoxically the only ground for genuine uniqueness. Without it, the individual talents of the members cannot be enjoyed and put in the service of the community. Instead they bring envy, injustice, odious comparison, the pitting against situations where one's self-worth is directly correlated with another's lack of it. Creaturehood is not leveling but the only foundation for a community in which variety can flourish.

Human limitation is a brute fact. As the existentialists say, we are thrown into existence without consultation and in most cases we shall be thrown out just as abruptly. Jesus' revelation of a forgiving Father urges us to accept this birth-death bound existence not as absurdity but as creaturehood. We are sons and daughters of the Father and we can live rightly and well within his creation. Limitation is a given; creaturehood is the free response and interpretation of that given. But the appropriation of our creaturehood, like trusting in God, does not happen with a single insight and a single decision. As the eschatological fervor of the early Church diminished, it quickly understood the process character of Christian life. The conversion to the life of Christ which baptism symbolized was not a once-and-for-all event. Under both external and internal pressure, people did not allow the Fatherhood of God to operate influentially in their lives. They fell from grace, sometimes dramatically but mostly out of negligence and forgetfulness. Heidegger talks about inauthenticity as the forgetfulness of Being. Sin is the forgetfulness of creaturehood. Part of the reason for the development of the sacrament of Penance was that people needed to be reminded of their true calling. Because humankind is free and time wears down our firmest resolutions, growth in creaturehood means not one experience of conversion but continual struggling responses to the Father of Jesus.

This growth process, how a person continues to experience divine forgiveness which calls him to full creaturehood, is the key to the spirituality of Jesus. The dynamic is best illustrated in the structure of the Our Father. The prayer begins by addressing God as Abba which means the person praying has experienced divine forgiveness and is confident and intimate with the Father. Although the person praying has experienced the Kingdom, a phrase later she asks "Thy Kingdom come." She places herself in the eschatological tension of Jesus. She prays that God's divine forgiveness which she initially and partially experienced will fully overtake and transform her life. The implicit question is, "How do I respond to the experience of divine forgiveness which cuts through my sin and calls forth my goodness?" The answer is in the phrase, "Forgive us our sins as we ourselves forgive those who have sinned against us." This is saying more than that we buy God's forgiveness by forgiving others. Humankind's relationship to God is more than shrewd business transaction. Also it means something deeper than that human forgiveness mirrors divine forgiveness. When we forgive our neighbor, we do more than reflect the fact that God forgives us. The fullest meaning of the petition is what Norman Perrin calls "contemporaneity of action."[13] Situated in the initial experience of God's forgiveness, humankind moves out in forgiveness to each other and in that very act enters more deeply into the experience of divine forgiveness. With this dynamic, Jesus interlocks God, self, and neighbor in an everlasting unity. We experience the divine call past *our* sins to *our* possibilities when we invite the neighbor's goodness. Any competition between God and neighbor for the energies and attentions of the self is a false fight. The good news is out. To trust, forgive, and love the neighbor is the path leading ever deeper into the trust, forgiveness, and love of God.

The Gospel writers portray Peter as Jesus' best foil. Since he never quite understood, his questions always penetrated to the heart of the matter. "Master how many times should I forgive my brother? Seven times?" Jesus' response is, "I tell you not seven times but seventy times seven." The evidence is overwhelming that we are enthusiastic and repeating violators of our own and each other's humanity. But we are more than that. If we are to live together, we must develop a style of forgiveness which can entice that more. We need a forgiveness which stares through the center of our sins and affirms the goodness we are capable of. Not to persist in forgiveness is quite clearly to give up, to wallow in the luxury of condemnation, to judge humankind to be stuck too deeply in the mire, and cry solemnly in our beer. But the Christian community, which is faithful to the God who forgives, knows that beer is for drinking, not crying into. The community which is true to Jesus will always hear and dance to the music of The Good Creation which rises above the cacophony of The Fall.

Chapter 7

The Challenge To Love

If love has the power to make the world go round, it can also bring it to a screaming halt. This seems to be the thrust of Rollo May's contention that love, which was once the answer to life's predicaments, is now the problem.[1] A life without love was once considered the worst fate that could befall a person. Yet today the question is: "What is this thing called love which makes life so livable?" Like most primal words, love collects feelings like ships collect barnacles. The same word which a husband whispers to his wife on their twenty-fifth wedding anniversary a child says to a puppy. But the contemporary problem with love goes deeper than "abuse by overuse," and the resulting semantic confusion. Abrubtly stated: Too many people feel too little. The opposite of love, which is pointed out by both Menninger and May, is not hatred but apathy. We cannot muster the driving affect necessary to live creatively with one another. We feel powerless to change our own lives and to influence others; so we become indifferent. As this defensive indifference hardens it works the revenge of isolating us. We approach the simple statement of living death, "I no longer care." Faced with this schizoid world (a society out of touch and unable to feel), Rollo May suggests we return to the source of love which hopefully will reinvigorate us.

To return to the source is a familiar journey for the religious person. In all of life's experiences, those smooth and those rocky, the religious person seeks funding and direction from the deepest ground of personal existence. This habit of returning to the source is neither an escape nor a solution. The religious person does not run there furtively looking back over his shoulder. He repairs there to consult larger purposes and reaffirm enduring values in order to act more creatively in the immediate frays of interpersonal and social living. The source does not promise magical solutions or the equivalent of the cowardly suggestion, "Close your eyes long enough and it will go away." Dwelling within the source brings insight and inspiration. Problems and situations are freshly perceived; consciousness is transformed. The pain does not go away but it is made bearable and, in some cases, creative of new life. Dwelling within the source paradoxically relativizes the importance of our problems while reaffirming the importance of us. In this context we come with our dwindling love and escalating indifference to Jesus, more precisely through Jesus to the source of all there is—the creative and redemptive God.

Life is so infinitely varied and experience so myriad that any attempt to catch it all in a single breath seems futile. Yet when we do attempt to see the world in a grain of sand, the grain of sand is usually love. What everything is about, the reductionist says, is our love or lack of it. Although this may be true, it appears too simple. Yet there is precedent. When the lawyer asked Jesus, "Master, what command is the greatest in the law?" he replied, "You must love the Lord your God with your whole heart, your whole soul and your whole mind. There is a second like it. You must love your neighbor as you do yourself. These two commands sum up the whole of the law and the prophets."[2] The endless intrigues of moral theology and the accumulated injunctions for lawful behavior are unabashedly confronted by the command of love. Christians throughout history have followed this lead of Jesus and used love to pull together the multiple strands of experience. John Wesley proclaimed God to be "pure unbounded Love" and the criterion of Christian life remains that of the Johannine Christ's, "By this love you have for one another everyone will know that you are my disciples."[3]

The double commandment to love takes on a different emphasis in each of the Synoptic Gospels.[4] In Matthew, the relationship of love to the law is stressed. The double commandment is not merely the preeminent injunction of the law but love of God and neighbor contain the whole law and provide the focus for interpreting the other commands. In Mark, the lawyer responds to Jesus' two commands by repeating them and adding that they are worth more than "all these burnt offerings and sacrifices."[5] Jesus approves of this addition and replies, "You are not far from the Kingdom of God." Mark is not unraveling the meaning of love but stressing the true nature of religion. What is important is obedience to the will of God and love for your fellow person, not cultic sacrifice. The Lukan rendition of the double commandment is the most provocative.[6] Luke combines the command to love with the parable of the Good Samaritan. In this setting, the Good Samaritan is transformed from a parable stressing the need to abandon all presuppositions in order to experience the Kingdom into an exemplary story. The double commandment to love can appear a romantic ideal and be embraced with much enthusiasm but little understanding. Luke brings rarified love crashingly to earth with the parable of the Good Samaritan. Love is as concrete, distasteful, and expensive as picking up a beaten man and nursing him back to health. As the parable relates the extent of the Samaritan's generosity the point is driven deeper into our own selfishness:

> He went up and bandaged his wounds, pouring oil and wine on them. He then lifted him on to his own mount, carried him to the inn and looked after him. Next day, he took out two denarii and handed them to the innkeeper. "Look after him," he said "and on my way back I will make good any extra expense you have."[7]

Love is not well-wishing but commitment to the other in need to the extent of our time, strength, and money.

Luke's juxtaposition of the double commandment and the parable of the Good Samaritan powerfully illustrates the style of Jesus. In the course of this short conversation with the questioning lawyer three radical and possibly redemptive changes occur. First, the challenger becomes the one challenged. The exchange begins with, "Then an expert in the law got up to test him [Jesus] and said, 'Master what must I do to make sure of eternal life?' " Jesus returned question for question, "What does the law say?" The lawyer states the double commandment and Jesus commends him but "he [the lawyer] wishing to justify his question asked, 'Who is my neighbor?' " Jesus' answer is the parable of the Good Samaritan ending with another question, "Which of these three do you think proved himself a neighbor to the man who fell into the robber's hands?" The reluctant but only answer is, "The man who took pity on him." The section ends with the imperative, "Go and do likewise." In this interchange more than information is involved; egos are at stake. The interchange begins with the insincere lawyer's routine challenge to this Galilean's knowledge and ends with Jesus radically challenging his behavior.

Second, the discussion moves from abstract law to an actual lived situation. Jesus refuses to dally with the intellectual question or to delight in the subtle intricacies of the law; he demands action. It is important to note in Luke's version that it is the lawyer who articulates the double commandment to love. Jesus' response is an abrupt, "All right, you know the law; now do it."

Third, the fact that it is a Samaritan who helps suggests that it is a Jew in need. There are four people in the parable and the lawyer, who is the listener, will identify with one of them. He cannot imagine himself as the priest and the Levite who pass by and certainly not the despised Samaritan. That leaves him bleeding and helpless by the side of the road. The lawyer is "that certain man on his way down from Jerusalem to Jericho." The lawyer has moved from prosecutor to defendant, from pursuing an intellectual question to confronting an actual situation, from a respected scholar to a robbed and beaten man. The Father's love mediated through his Son is confronting and calling the lawyer to actually love his neighbor.

The lawyer, imaginatively abandoned and bleeding, is driven to realize the full meaning of the command to love your neighbor as yourself. With that awesome impact which only parables are capable of, he realizes that every time he passes by the man in the ditch, he is passing himself by. The ingenuity, passion, and wholeheartedness with which he pursues his own welfare must be the ingenuity, passion, and wholeheartedness with which he pursues his neighbor's welfare. Knowing the depth of our self-love Jesus' command is that we must love our neighbor no less. Kierkegaard expands on how adroitly this simple phrase "as oneself" infiltrates our egoism and paradoxically robs us of it:

> If we are to love our neighbour as ourselves, then this commandment opens, as with a master-key, the lock of our self-love and snatches it away from us. Should the commandment to love our neighbor be formulated in another way than by the expression as thyself, which can be handled so easily and yet has the tension of all eternity, the commandment could not master our self-love so effectively.

The meaning of as thyself cannot be twisted and turned; judging man with the insight of eternity, it penetrates the innermost part of his soul, where his egoism resides. It does not allow our egoism to make the least excuse, nor to evade it in any way. What a wonderful thing! One might have made longer penetrating speeches about the way man should love his neighbour, but again and again our egoism would have managed to produce excuses and evasions, because the matter would not have been completely exhausted, a certain aspect would have been passed over, a point would not have been described precisely enough or would not have been sufficiently binding in its expression. This as thyself however—truly, no wrestler could clasp his opponent more firmly or inextricably than this commandment clasps our egoism.[8]

But the command to love your neighbor as yourself is more than a clever trap leaving no room for escape. It intimates, although never states outright, that love involves a person in the life of another to the point of identification.

The Good Samaritan parable not only brings an in-depth understanding of what "as oneself" means but radically extends the concept of neighbor. It must have been painful to admit that if the Samaritan proved neighbor, there was no non-neighbor. The lawyer's question, "Who is my neighbor?" expected a lawyer's definition. The neighbor is, for example, he who pays tithes and visits the temple or he who resides within five miles of your home or he who is kinsman to you. The parable implies that if a Samaritan is neighbor to a Jew, every person is neighbor to every other. Cultural background, religious persuasion, or ethnic origin does not define neighbor. Neighbor is the next person met, especially those in need, and we must respond in love and service. As at other times, Jesus is proclaiming a universalism which breaks down artificial societal barriers and judges on the bedrock of common creaturehood.

Jesus' double commandment to love is a difficult ethic. It stretches the boundary of human selfhood to include the neighbor and fights against Satan's cynical evaluation of humankind in the Book of Job: "Skin only suffers when skin grieves."[9] The love of Jesus, however, does not stop with the robbed man on the side of the road but goes to the scandalous extreme of embracing the robbers. Matthew was afraid his listeners would understand Jesus in the Deuteronomic sense of loving your neighbor but hating your enemy. So he directly pits Jesus' command against Hebrew custom: "You have learnt how it was said: You must love your neighbour and hate your enemy. But I say this to you: love your enemies and pray for those who persecute you."[10] Luke plays off Jesus' insistence that we must love our enemies with the current Hellenistic golden rule that we return in kind:

> If you love those who love you, what thanks can you expect? Even sinners love those who love them. And if you do good to those who do good to you, what thanks can you expect? For even sinners do that much. And if you lend to those from whom you hope to receive, what thanks can you expect? Even sinners lend to sinners to get back the same amount. Instead, love your enemies and do good, and lend without any hope of return.[11]

With the injunction to love our enemies Jesus has fallen from the category of sage and teacher into that of God's fool.

In Jesus' vision, the motivation for loving our enemies is disturbingly simple. We are sons and daughters of the Most High who makes the rain fall on the good and the evil and the sun shine on the just and the unjust. If God loves all humankind, even those who are his enemies; we must do the same. This motivation for love is reflected in the fact that love is a commandment and not merely a suggestion. Love as commandment means that ultimately it arises from a source outside the self and the neighbor. For Jesus, love does not always have to stem from feelings within the self or from the attractiveness and lovability of the neighbor. We love the enemy, which means more than just not hating him or avoiding open conflict, because God loves him and we are God's. Love, in Jesus' ethic, may well be a feeling and attitude but it goes beyond that to be an act of the will which seeks the well being of every person.

Love your enemies is a hard saying and we soften it in many ways. We say that Jesus is an eschatological prophet who expected an imminent end to this mixed world of good and evil. Loving enemies was a short-term project with a big-time payoff in the near future. The Kingdom would soon arrive and those with love in their hearts would enter it. The injunction to love enemies was practical advice not to become preoccupied with retaliation but to keep your lamps burning, ready for the advent of the Judge. When it is obvious that we must live our entire lives with maliciousness and ambiguity, a more practical ethic is needed. Nonresistance would be overwhelmed by evil. Certainly, enemies must be loved and commended to God but also they must be fought or they will commend us to God. When faced with a cataclysmic end, humankind may beat swords into plowshares. But when the apocalypse is over, what returns, in the current jargon of the newscaster, is the "resumption of hostilities."

A second softener of the command to love your enemies might be characterized as "loving disinterest." The love of God is often said to be agape, a total outpouring which does not set its heart on response. The love which Jesus mediates into human affairs does not look to transform the enemy into a friend. It has no ambition, seeks no reconciliation, and is not moved by rejection. It is an enduringly gracious but disinterested presence which comes dangerously close to yawning. Can this noble and aloof love belong to the jealous God who desires Israel and who fulminates at her adulteries or the Jesus who weeps over unrepentant Jerusalem? Agape manages to give without risking and to be concerned without caring. If we are to use the human analogy of love for God's relationship to us, must we halve it to protect what we consider God's impassibility? Humankind wants return; we want to be kissed back; and in this respect God is like us. Even though primarily faithful to himself, God is not supremely indifferent when someone turns his back. The truth, which the stoical approach builds on but distorts, is that even when God's love is spurned, it is not taken away. God is adamant in loving humankind. He refuses to allow non-response to stop the free flow of his love and turn him from his creation. But stressing the permanence of God's commitment to us does not mean he is immune to our coldness and lack of hospitality. So "doing good to those who persecute you" cannot turn for protection to stoic indifference, a "who cares, I've done my thing" attitude. Jesus does not go to the cross unaffected by the rejection of the people, the betrayal of Judas, and the denial of Peter; but faced with this non-response, he continues to extend love. It is only honest to recognize that in not loving our enemies we hedge on Jesus. It is too facile to turn him into a mistaken apocalyptic or a passionless lover who does not hope for response, and so emasculate the man who had the courage to act in God's stead.

As with celebration, trust, and forgiveness, love leads into the Jesus dynamic of God, self, and neighbor. This dynamic is vividly portrayed in the farewell discourse of St. John's Gospel. The scene begins with the comment that Jesus "loved his own who were in the world."[12] In the light of Johannine Christology the love of Jesus must be understood as the love of the Father who sent him into the world and whom he, as Son, reveals. Jesus shows this love for his own by washing their feet. This enacted parable explains that the response to God's love is to love and serve the other. Then the scene concludes with Jesus' new commandment, "Love one another; just as I have loved you, you must love one another."[13] Jesus in his service to humankind is the model of responding to the love of God. The Christian life of love and service will run counter to the style of the introverted world and will be difficult to persevere in. In chapter fifteen, Jesus states, "Just as the Father has loved me so I have loved you. Abide in my love."[14] Abiding does not mean shelter but remaining in the supportive love of the Father and Jesus and thereby continuing to love and serve the neighbor. In this Johannine context, the interrelationship of the double commandment is revealed. God first loves us and rejoicing in this love we respond by loving our neighbor. The love of neighbor is not "beautiful dreams" but the harsh and dreadful reality which Dostoevski proclaimed. It means pursuing each person's well being, serving the enemy who may not respond but who will be loved because the sons and daughters are commissioned, by the birthright of their own experience of divine love, to bear forth in the world the universal love of the Father.

The contemporary person seeking the source of love will probably not be attracted to this vision of loving God and neighbor which Jesus proclaims. The assurance that the last power of existence is love is consoling—if you can believe it. The love-vision of Jesus is grounded in faith (every vision is) and the risk-taking necessary for faithful living is scarce in modern society. But faith, no matter how crucial, is not the major problem. It is not Jesus' revelation that God is love which makes us hesitate but his insistence on what this means. If God's love meant we must only pray and worship him, we would pray and worship him. If God's love meant that we must love him back (whoever and wherever he may be), we would love him back. But when God's love means wholehearted love and service of our neighbor, we stop. Something is wrong. Love should mean human fulfillment but this radical commitment to the well-being of the neighbor seems to imply the disillusion of the self. The other-centeredness of Jesus' love ethic is certainly commendable but a bit too heroic and forgetful of self to have real appeal. In a society which looks to love for fulfillment the message of self-sacrifice is bad news.

It cannot be denied that the theme of self-renunciation plays a major role in Christian history. Many saints seem to say they want nothing but to be nothing. Christian love is portrayed as exclusively agapistic, a pitcher endlessly pouring out and never needing to be refilled. In the purgative stage of spiritual growth, pride, understood as any reference to the self, must be burned away. The three religious vows—poverty, chastity and obedience—are attempts to devoid the self in order that God and the neighbor may be fully loved. Martin Luther says it succinctly, "I will do nothing in this life except what I see is necessary, profitable, and salutary to my neighbor."[15] Kierkegaard can always be counted on for a forceful presentation:

> The Christian self-denial thinks: give up your selfish wishes and desires, give up your selfish plans and purposes in order to work for the good in true disinterestedness—and then prepare to find yourself, just on that account, hated, scorned and mocked, and even executed as a criminal; or rather, do not prepare to find yourself in this situation, for that may become necessary, but choose it of your own free will. For Christian self-denial knows beforehand that these things will happen, and chooses them freely.[16]

This spirituality tends to think any sign of self-concern is a sign of original sin.

Despite the history of Christian witness, self-renouncing love is deeply questionable and sometimes a shade too fond of suffering. Can a person really pursue the well-being of another when she is so heedless of her own well-being? Asking people to stretch their skins to include the neighbor is one thing but asking them to leave their skins behind is another. Overcoming self-concern, even if it were desirable, is (excuse the pun) a self-defeating project. The attempt to dissolve the self either turns passionately morbid and smacks of Manichaeism or proves as ultimately laughable as the attempts to escape sexuality. The cynic notices the incongruity when the high calling of self-abasement is talked about. There can be a hidden selfish heart to Christian sacrificial love—you totally serve God and neighbor in order that you might be saved. Self-concern is still master of the house.

Yet Christian love demands a sacrifice. But what must be given up is not the self but the ego. The presence of Christian love is a movement from the dissolution of the ego to the expansion of the self. This movement is mapped in the classical Christological hymn to God's love:

His state was divine,
yet he did not cling
to his equality with God
but emptied himself
to assume the condition of a slave,
and became as men are;
and being as all men are,
he was humbler yet,
even to accepting death,
death on a cross.

> But God raised him high
> and gave him the name
> which is above all other names
> so that all beings
> in the heavens, on earth and in the underworld,
> should bend the knee at the name of Jesus
> and that every tongue should acclaim
> Jesus Christ as Lord,
> to the glory of God the Father.[17]

This hymn details what theologians call kenosis, the emptying out of God into human nature. The text is a quagmire where many an exegete has gone under and the interpretations are legion. The popular flavor has always been that the Son gave up the soft life of a sky god to become humankind's crucified savior. For our purposes, the key line (variously translated) is, "Yet he did not cling to his equality with God." Whatever its function in the hymn, this line intimates that a "clung-to divinity" ceases to be divinity. The nature of true divinity is the outward embracement of all beings. A God who stands on his prerogative and protects his rights at all costs is a false god. This god has subordinated his true selfhood to ego. The ego is the self turned inward, preoccupied and anxious about its status. Only when the ego is dissolved can the self move outward in genuine presence to the other. With this understanding, kenosis, the self-emptying of God, is also paradoxically his self-becoming.

If the love of God dissolved the ego and expanded the self to include humankind, the Christian is urged to participate in the same dynamic. The clung-to self is the ego isolated and invulnerable. The ego spends time and energy on elaborate strategies of protection, anguishes over blemishes and bruises, and plots its solitary survival. Christian love is the suggestive word of the Lord to let go. Clinging gives the feeling of security but it is really only the safety of a prison. In this Christian context, May and Menninger must go a step further. The deepest root of non-love is not apathy but ego pity, a desperate, sorrowing hold on selfhood. The Christian traditions are unanimous in affirming that genuine love entails sacrifice. At root, what is sacrificed is the ego so that the self may be free.

The movement of Christian love which breaks down the constricting defenses of the ego and allows the self to include the other as person is a genuine process of growth. It is grounded in John Donne's realization that no man is an island. To exist is to coexist; to be a person is to be a fellow-person; to develop is to interact. The reason the contemporary "inability to relate" causes so much anxiety is that it is not one activity among many but the essense of who we are. The self is a becoming which wills to belong to other people and grow with them. In order to belong, the self must communicate to give itself to the other. Conversely, the self must receive the gifts of communication from the others. In the interaction of giving and receiving the self learns a love which is not possessive and which respects the distinctiveness and freedom of the other person. The self expands from the solitary "I" to the collective "We." It identifies with the other and in some sense "becomes the other."

Love is always prone to exaggeration. And nowhere is this more true than in the area of identifi-

cation. Identification grates on common sense because it is often interpreted as absorption. The lover
becomes the beloved; the self is lost in the other; I
am my neighbor. This total-love alchemy, turning
into another, does not respect the non-fluidity of
the self and definite "non-me-ness" of all other
people. Yet within love there is the experience of
conscious participation in the life of the other. This
does not mean that I share the very being of the
beloved but that person's joy and suffering, success
and failure are somehow mine. I am related to that
person in such a way that although my life remains
mine and her life hers, I experience the activities of
her life as mine. Identification of this kind is behind
the Judgment scene in Matthew where Jesus says of
those who have helped their fellowpersons, "I was
hungry and you gave me to eat. I was thristy and
you gave me to drink, etc."[18] The extensions of the
self in love grounds Jesus' remarks to Saul who was
persecuting Christians on the road to Damascus.
"Saul, Saul why are you persecuting me?"[19] We do
not have to retreat into mysticism to understand
Jesus' identification with the early Church. It is an
outgrowth of that magnificent line of St. John's Last
Discourse, "Jesus . . . loved his own to the end."[20]
The Jerusalem Bible comments simply on this
verse, "i.e. utterly."

The Christian loves first. This means he is biased;
his stance is a fundamental openness to the person-
hood of the other. This prejudice, which is prior to
all knowledge and every situation, is in imitation of
the love of God revealed in Jesus. The doctrine of
God's love which leaves theologians, after torrents

of words, slackjawed, is the Incarnation. With the kenosis text, the emphasis is on the expansion of the self. God has not remained in spendid isolation, the Perfect One, impassable and sovereign. He has poured himself into history, taken flesh and risked himself in the hands of reckless humankind. Although we do not have to agree with Altizer and insist on the total collapse of the transcendent God into the immanence of time and history, we must not back off the radical implications of God's enfleshment. Often theologians, fearful of losing God's transcendence, deny him, with the subtle distinctions of a monolithic metaphysics, the flesh he has freely taken. Docetism is a heresy with a thousand faces. God shares our human existence and when our psyches crack and our bodies break, he suffers. When in love and freedom we release each other from our fears, heal our wounds, and build the beloved community; he rejoices with us. We have no right to deny God our pain and hope, for we are part of him. Charles Hartshorne has theologically captured the extent of the Incarnation with the term "panentheism." This does not mean that the world is God but the world is in God. God's love has extended his selfhood to include all of creation. Hartshorne has a magnificent passage on God's involvement in human existence:

> God orders the universe . . . by taking into his own life all the currents of feeling in existence. He is the most irresistible of influences precisely because he is himself the most open to influence. In the depths of their hearts all creatures (even those able to 'rebel' against him) defer to God because they sense him as the one who alone is adequately moved by

what moves them. He alone not only knows but feels . . . how they feel, and he finds his own joy in sharing their lives, lived according to their own free decisions, not fully anticipated by any detailed plan of his own. Yet the extent to which they can be permitted to work out their own plan depends on the extent to which they can echo or imitate on their own level the divine sensitiveness to the needs and precious freedom of all . . . This [is a] vision of a deity who is not a supreme autocrat, but a universal agent of 'persuasion,' whose 'power is the worship he inspires'. . . .[21]

The Incarnation does not tell all of God's love. Bethlehem might be construed as a gesture; Golgotha is irrevocable commitment. We can fantasize about God, paint technicolor heavens, and recite the wide-eyed legends of spectacular interventions but when we are disillusioned with our dreams, we must come, as Tyrrell said, to "That strange Man upon the Cross."[22] The human face of God is the strangulating Jesus stretched against the sky, vulnerable to taunts and lances. We busy ourselves with the question, "Why did God let his son die?" and construct theories of atonement which neither excuse nor explain. The answer, without flirting with Patripassianism, is that God could not rescue Jesus for he was on the cross with him. The inclusion of humankind into the selfhood of God in the person of Jesus extends to the extremities of human existence. God's love is not about supernatural rescue but divine sharing in human suffering. Bonhoeffer has intimated, the God whose investment in humankind means nails for him is the only God who counts. He is the God whose blood resists facile psychologizing and whose

death refutes the might of the world. On the acceptance or rejection of this God, the Suffering One,
hangs the meaning of existence. An old Polish Jew
who had been through the massacre of the Warsaw
ghetto and converted to Christianity, looks at the
crucified Christ: "As I looked at that man upon the
cross, . . . I knew I must make up my mind once
and for all, and either take my stand beside him and
share in his undefeated faith in God . . . or else fall
finally into a bottomless pit of bitterness, hatred,
and unutterable despair."[23]

Nietzsche has suggested that we are too obtuse,
set in our ways, and downright fearful of what God
on the cross means. If we would open ourselves to
the event of Christ, all our values would be transformed. Perfection and the good life would no
longer be conceived as invulnerability. Suffering
love would replace aloof indifference. Human activity would not be fortress building, the amassing of
wealth and power to fend off the ravages of time,
but bridge-building, the sharing of common existence. The cross of Christ initially seen as com-
promising God's power under the influence of the
Spirit was eventually understood as the revelation
of true power. When conceptions of God built on
worldy empire and sovereign prestige are dragged
to the cross for affirmation, they are revealed as
projections of humankind's worst instincts. Whitehead remarks that God is not a ruling Caesar or a
ruthless moralist or an unmoved mover. The Christian story dwells "upon the tender elements in the
world, which slowly and in quietness operate by
love; and it finds purpose in the present immediacy

of a kingdom not of this world. Love neither rules, nor is it unmoved; also it is a little oblivious as to morals." This suggests another important aspect of the relationship between God and humankind which is revealed in the cross. God's nonresistance has absolute and total respect for human freedom. He solicits human goodness but will not force it. He calls the mind to truth but will not compel it to obey. Humankind may be determined by genes, environment, and its own fears but not by God. The death of Christ upon the cross reveals what God values above all else—human freedom. Human freedom will not be co-opted, even if it chooses to kill the Son. The cross of Christ tells us more about Ultimate Reality and more about human responsibility than we care to know.

The fact that God broke his ego isolation and expanded his selfhood to the point of identifying with humankind in its negativity does not mean he seeks suffering. Cruelty and terrifying death are not the plan of God but the doings of humankind. There is nothing inevitable about the cross, as some atonement theories contend. When the cross is seen as the preordained means by which humankind is redeemed, God is implicated in the death of Christ not as fellowsufferer but as executioner. Humankind spills the blood of God and its own blood not because it is acting out a redemptive ritual but because we will have it no other way. It is inconsistent, if not unreal, to recognize situations as basically open to human determination and then to construe the death of Christ as a necessary event for time, history, and cosmos. God suffers pain and death in our world not because he loves suffering and sees it as intrinsically valuable; but because he loves us and if we persist in crucifying each other, he will share it rather than go away. The mystery of God and humankind on the cross goes on. Perhaps when we realize that God's love everlastingly binds him to us and all the evil we can muster will not break that tie, we might take both him and ourselves down.

So Christian love, like the love of God revealed in the crucified Christ, breaks egoism and expands the self to include the neighbor or, perhaps more precisely put, the enlarged self-neighbor. It does not pursue pain and suffering to test its selflessness and neighbor-centeredness. It understands this is a false dichotomy which does not realize that all well-being is mutual. But pain and suffering may come. Situations may arise where the only path of non-pain is to retreat to egoism. In a fallen world, sometimes the only way to stay alive is to abandon the neighbor. The Christian understands this as false life, life clung to at the price of love, life not worth living. Christian love demands fidelity to the expanded self-neighbor, even though it mean death. The agony in the garden shows that Christ does not invite the cross but accepts it rather than abandon the Kingdom and the neighbor. In an age which accuses the Christian of being a nay-sayer it is important to understand that the love-command to lay down one's life for a friend is not self-denial but fidelity to the enlarged self-neighbor. In either-or situations not to lay down your life is not only to abandon the neighbor but to betray who you are. This insight, when we abandon God or neighbor what we really lose is ourself, is portrayed in Robert Bolt's play *A Man For All Seasons*. Thomas More explains to his daughter that to take the oath and abandon God would be to lose himself:

> When a man takes an oath, Meg, he's holding his own self in his own hands. Like water. (He cups his hands) And if he opens his fingers then—he needn't hope to find himself again.[25]

She argues that it is not his fault that the state is three-quarters bad and if he elects to suffer for it, he is also electing himself a hero. He sees it differently:

> That's very neat. But look now . . . If we lived in a State where virtue was profitable, common sense would make us good, and greed would make us saintly. And we'd live like animals or angels in the happy land that needs no heroes. But since in fact we see that avarice, anger, envy, pride, sloth, lust and stupidity commonly profit far beyond humility, chastity, fortitude, justice and thought, and have to choose, to be human at all . . . why then perhaps we must stand fast a little—even at the risk of being heroes.[26]

Christian love is neither heroic nor romantic but in an ambiguous world it attempts "to stand fast a little." This fidelity to love which means physical death the Christian knows as Resurrection.

The love which Jesus challenges us to is the love which enlarges God to include humankind and the self to include the neighbor. Also, at the insistence of Jesus this love cannot remain visionary. It must be concretely practised. The theology of love urges us to learn the skills of love. How do we care for each other interpersonally in ways which do not suffocate and oppress? How is the well-being of the neighbor pursued in the complex problem of global hunger and international war? How are communities developed positively around respect and care for each person rather than around a common enemy? How are the systemic causes of non-love eliminated? These questions and myriad others require creative human endeavor and the only answers seem to be those which are reformulated and ever-open to improvement. But the Christ on the cross will not allow us to slip into ego and forget the question. His crucified flesh is the everpresent insistence: God loves us and we must love each other.

Enthusiasts are always bothersome. They rush about with their message, blatantly proselytizing, disgustingly happy, and, in general, disrupting the efficient running of the world. Yet of all mongers, the love monger is the easiest to forgive. Love does not say everything about us but it may say the most important thing. It may say the way-down feeling of joy we somethings have which is so overwhelming that we become afraid and dismiss it with, "That's too good to be true." But love just might be what the impenetrable mystery of God, self, and neighbor is all about and if it is, kill the fatted calf and call in the musicians. One can understand Paul's rapture:

> If I have all the eloquence of men or of angels, but speak without love, I am simply a gong booming or a cymbal clashing. If I have the gift of prophecy, understanding all the mysteries there are, and knowing everything, and if I have faith in all its fullness, to move mountains, but without love, then I am nothing at all. If I give away all that I

possess, piece by piece, and if I even let them take my body to burn it, but am without love, it will do me no good whatever.

Love is always patient and kind; it is never jealous; love is never boastful or conceited; it is never rude or selfish; it does not take offense, and is not resentful. Love takes no pleasure in other people's sins but delights in the truth; it is always ready to excuse, to trust, to hope, and to endure whatever comes.

Love does not come to an end. But if there are gifts of prophecy, the time will come when they must fail; or the gift of languages, it will not continue forever; and knowledge—for this, too, the time will come when it must fail. For our knowledge is imperfect and our prophesying is imperfect; but once perfection comes, all imperfect things will disappear. When I was a child, I used to talk like a child, and think like a child, and argue like a child, but now I am a man, all childish ways are put behind me. Now we are seeing a dim reflection in a mirror; but then we shall be seeing face to face. The knowledge that I have now is imperfect; but then I shall know as fully as I am known.

In short, there are three things that last: faith, hope and love; and the greatest of these is love.[27]

Footnotes
Chapter One

[1]Flannery O'Connor, *Wise Blood*. New York: Signet Books, 1964, p. 16

[2]Ignazio Silone, "What Remains: A Word about Socialism and Christianity," *Encounter*, XXXI, December, 1968, p. 62.

[3]Robertson Davies, *Fifth Business*. New York: Viking Press, 1970, pp. 135-36.

[4]Luke 12:51

[5]Luke 22:36

[6]Matthew 26:53

[7]Harvey Cox, *A Feast of Fools*. Cambridge: Harvard University Press, 1969, pp. 140-41.

[8]Leander Keck, *A Future for the Historical Jesus*. Nashville and New York: Abingdon Press, 1971, p. 104.

[9]This image, of course, is not without its propagandistic uses. It has often been brought in to shore up the sagging authoritative timbers of the Church. The Divine Founder has passed on his infallible perception and judgment to the hierarchial leaders.

186 The Challenge of Jesus

Chapter Two

¹Wallace Stevens, "The Man with the Blue Guitar", *The Collected Poems of Wallace Stevens*. New York: Alfred A. Knopf, Inc., 1954, p. 165.

²Bruce Vawter, *This Man Jesus*. New York: Doubleday & Company, 1973, p. 33.

³Mark 6:5-6

⁴Matthew 13:58

⁵Luke 24:26

⁶Van Harvey, *The Historian and the Believer*. New York: The Macmillan Company, 1969, pp. 265-268.

⁷Ibid., p. 266.

⁸Ibid., p. 267.

⁹John Dominic Crossan, *In Parables*. New York: Harper & Row, Publishers, 1973, p. 33.

¹⁰Leander Keck, *A Future for the Historical Jesus*. Nashville and New York: Abingdon Press, 1971, pp. 243-265.

¹¹John 1:37-40

¹²John 14:6

¹³Quoted in S. Paul Schilling, *God in an Age of Atheism*. Nashville and New York: Abingdon Press, 1969, p. 86.

¹⁴John Paul Sartre, *Nausea*. New York: A New Directions Paperbook, 1964, pp. 170, 171, 174, 175, 180.

¹⁵Avery Dulles, *Testimonial to Grace*. New York: Sheed and Ward, 1946, pp. 51, 65.

¹⁶Cf. Andrew Greeley, *Ecstasy, A Way of Knowing*. New Jersey: Prentice-Hall, Inc., 1974.

¹⁷Abraham Maslow, "Religious Aspects of Peak-experiences," *Personality and Religion*, ed. William A. Sadler, Jr. New York: Harper & Row, Publishers, 1970, p. 179.

¹⁸Psalm 33:6

¹⁹Isaiah 55:10-11

Chapter Three

[1]Karl Menninger, *Whatever Became of Sin?* New York: Hawthorn Books, Inc. 1973, p. 2.

[2]John 2:23

[3]Romans 7:15

[4]John 3:18

[5]Isaiah 6:5

[6]Luke 5:8

[7]Luke 18:8

[8]Luke 11:20

[9]Matthew 4:3

[10]Mark 5:7

[11]Matthew 16:16

[12]Luke 22:70

[13]Mark 15:39

[14]Exodus 17:7

[15]John 10:36-38

[16]John 14:9

[17]Cf. Warren F. Groff, *Christ the Hope of the Future: Signals of a Promised Humanity.* Grand Rapids, Michigan: William B. Eerdmans Publishing Company, 1971. pp. 88-121.

[18]Luke 2:52

[19]John Cobb, "A Whiteheadian Christology," in *Process Philosophy and Christian Thought.* Edited by Delwin Brown, Ralph E. James, Jr., and Gene Reeves. New York: The Bobbs-Merrill Company, Inc., 1971, pp. 382-398.

[20]R.H. Fuller, *The New Testament in Current Study.* London: SCM Press, 1962, p. 43.

[21]Cobb, op. cit., p. 393.

[22]Matthew 16:23

[23]Mark 14:36

[24]John Donne in an interview in *The National Catholic Reporter.*

[25]David Griffin, "Schubert Ogden's Christology and the Possibilities of Process Philosophy," in *Process Philosophy and Christian Thought.* op. cit., p. 353.

[26]Paul Tillich, *Systematic Theology,* Vol. I. Chicago: The University of Chicago Press, 1951, p. 13.

[27]Theodore Roszak, *Where the Wasteland Ends.* New York: Doubleday, 1972, p. 136.

[28]Erich Fromm, *The Revolution of Hope.* New York: Bantam Books, 1968, p. 54.

[29]Psalm 115:3-8

[30]Langdon Gilkey, *Shantung Compound The Story of Men and Women under Pressure.* New York: Harper & Row, 1966, p. 74.

[31]Ibid., p. 230.

[32]Ibid., p. 233.

[33]Ibid., p. 234.

Chapter Four

[1]Matthew 6:16

[2]Nicolas Berdyaev, *The Meaning of the Creative Act*. New York: Collier Books, 1962, p. 238.

[3]Ernst Kasemann, *Jesus Means Freedom*. Philadelphia: Fortress Press, 1968, p. 64.

[4]Quoted by Carl E. Braaten, *Christ and Counter-Christ*. Philadelphia: Fortress Press, 1972, p. 96.

[5]Unpublished poem, "The Hour of the Unexpected," by John Shea.

[6]Matthew 11:19

[7]Matthew 9:14-15

[8]Luke 15:6

[9]Luke 15:32

[10]Matthew 6:25-34

[11]Walter Kerr, *Tragedy and Comedy*. New York: Simon and Schuster, 1968, p. 144.

[12]Romans 8:38-39

[13]Quoted in Langdon Gilkey, *Maker of Heaven and Earth*. New York: Doubleday, 1959, p. 253.

[14]Matthew 10:28

[15]Romans 14:8

[16]John 16:33

[17]Unpublished poem, "After the End," by John Shea.

[18]John A.T. Robinson, *The New Reformation*. Philadelphia: The Westminster Press, p. 36.

[19]Mark 8:31

[20]Luke 12:8

[21]Bruce Vawter, *This Man Jesus*. New York: Doubleday, 1973, p. 106.

[22]Daniel 7:9-10, 7:13-14

[23]Quoted by Geoffrey Ainger, *Jesus Our Contemporary*. London: SCM Press, 1967, p. 49.

Chapter Five

[1]Rm. 5:19

[2]John L. McKenzie, *The Power and the Wisdom*. Milwaukee: The Bruce Publishing Company, 1965, p. 92.

[3]Paul Ricoeur, *The Symbolism of Evil*. Boston: Beacon Press, 1967, pp. 232-306.

[4]The story of the Fall. Genesis 3:1-24

[5]Robert Nesbet, *Community and Power*. Galaxy edition, p. viii.

[6]Andrew Greeley, *The Catholic Manifesto*. New York: Doubleday, forthcoming.

[7]Albert Camus, *The Stranger*. New York: Vintage Books, 1946, p. 1.

[8]G. K. Chesterton, *Orthodoxy*. Garden City Publishing, p. 294.

[9]Quoted by Maurice Friedman, *To Deny Our Nothingness*. New York: A Delta Book, 1967, p. 17.

[10]Luke 4:13

[11]Mark 14:36

[12]Mark 15:34

[13]Psalm 21:27-31

[14]Mark 10:15

[15]To make God an androgyne, a mythical man-woman, must be distinguished from the legitimate emphasis on the need to develop the feminine-masculine aspects of every personality and incorporate this "fuller" notion of person into every God symbol.

[16]Cf. Norman Perrin, *Rediscovering the Teaching of Jesus*. New York: Harper & Row, Publishers, 1967, pp. 125-126.

[17]Luke 22:33

[18]Luke 22:62

[19]Quoted in James F. Childress, "Nonviolent Resistance: Trust and Risk-Taking," JRE. 1/1 (1973), p. 100.

[20]Seward Hiltner, *Theological Dynamics*. New York: Abingdon Pess, 1972, pp. 70-71.

[21]Leander Keck, *A Future for the Historical Jesus*. Nashville and New York: Abingdon Press, 1971, pp. 240-1.

[22]John 13:3-5

Chapter Six

[1]As quoted by Roland H. Bainton, *Here I Stand: A Life of Martin Luther.* New York: New American Library, 1955, p. 31.

[2]As quoted in F.W. Dillistone, *The Christian Understanding of Atonement.* Philadelphia: The Westminster Press, 1968, p. 29.

[3]Luke 17:20

[4]Luke 15:20-21

[5]Joachim Jeremias, *Rediscovering the Parables.* New York: Charles Scribner's Sons, 1966, p. 102.

[6]Luke 15:22-24

[7]Luke 19:1-10

[8]Richard Ray, "Appreciation and Distaste: A Focus on the Aesthetics of Human Affirmation," *Union Seminary Quarterly Review.* Vol. XXVII, No. 4. Summer, 1972, p. 218.

[9]Cf. Norman Perrin, *Rediscovering the Teaching of Jesus.* New York: Harper & Row, Publishers, 1967, p. 94.

[10]John 18:28

[11]Jeremias, op. cit., p. 115-16.

[12]John 11:50

[13]Perrin, op. cit., p. 152.

Chapter Seven

[1]Rollo May, *Love and Will*. New York: W.W. Norton & Company, 1969, p. 13.

[2]Matthew 22:36-40

[3]John 13:35

[4]Cf. Victor Paul Furnish, *The Love Command in the New Testament*. Nashville and New York: Abingdon Press, 1972.

[5]Mark 12:28-34

[6]Luke 10:25-37

[7]Luke 10: 34-36

[8]Quoted by Gunther Bornkamm, *Jesus of Nazareth*. New York: Harper & Row, Publishers, 1960, p. 113-14.

[9]Job 2:4

[10]Matthew 5:43-44

[11]Luke 6:31-35

[12]John 13:1

[13]John 13:33

[14]John 15:9

[15]Quoted in Daniel Day Williams, *The Spirit and the Forms of Love*. New York: Harper & Row, Publishers, 1968, p. 197.

[16]Ibid., p. 199.

[17]Philippians 2:6-11

[18]Matthew 25:31-46

[19]Acts 9:4

[20]John 13:1

[21]As quoted in Gordon D. Kaufman, *Systematic Theology: A Historicist Perspective*. New York: Charles Scribner's Sons, 1968, p. 213.

[22]As quoted in W. Norman Pittenger, *The Word Incarnate*. Digsell Place: James Nisbet & Co. LTD, 1959, p. 10.

[23]S. Paul Schilling, *God in an Age of Atheism*. Nashville and New York: Abingdon Press, 1969, p. 187.

[24]Alfred North Whitehead, *Process and Reality*. New York: The Macmillan Company, 1929, p. 521.

[25]Robert Bolt, *A Man For All Seasons*. New York: Random House, 1960, p. 140.

[26]Ibid., pp. 140-1.

[27]1 Cor. 13:1-13